KU-072-074

vc poker.com

THE COMPLETE GUIDE TO
POKER

THE WORLD'S BEST POKER WRITERS
REVEAL THEIR SECRETS

IN ASSOCIATION WITH

vc poker.com

EDITORIAL

EDITOR **James Hipwell**
ART EDITOR **Spike McCormack**
MANAGING EDITOR **Pete Walker**
DESIGNERS **Gwyn Calley, Wayne Middleton, Sarah-Jane Mortimer**
SUB EDITORS **Julie Alpine, Kirsty Fortune**

CONTRIBUTORS

Paul Cheung, Nolan Dalla, Andrew NS Glazer, James Hipwell, Phil Shaw, James Tye, Professor Leighton Vaughan Williams, Roland de Wolfe

IMAGES

Danny Bird, Kevin February, Ian McKinnell, Tom Miles, Movie Store Collection, Anthony Rule, Carole Tuff

PUBLISHING & MARKETING

MANAGING DIRECTOR **James Tye**
020 7907 6289
PUBLISHER **Richard Downey**
020 7907 6488
COMMERCIAL MANAGER **Emily Ford**
020 7907 6349
MARKETING MANAGER **Claire Childs**
020 7907 6113
LIST RENTAL MANAGER **Nerys Church**
020 7907 6140
ACCOUNTS DIRECTOR **Martin Belson**
020 7907 6150

WHAT IS *INSIDEEDGE?*
All the articles in this bookazine were either first published in *InsideEdge* magazine or written specifically by *InsideEdge* for this publication. *InsideEdge* is the UK's biggest and best gambling mag.

Launched in 2004, *InsideEdge* is the magazine of choice for the discerning gambler. Offering both strategy and expert advice, as well as top tips, it's a must-read for anyone looking to improve their gambling results.

All major sports events are covered, as well as casino and poker advice, in a way that's both entertaining and accessible. At *InsideEdge* we deliver advice in a way that recreates the buzz and excitement involved in placing a bet. Call 0845 644 0239 to subscribe or go to *www.subsinfo.co.uk/insideedge* for all the latest offers.

SUBSCRIPTION BUREAU **0845 644 0239**
BACK ISSUES **01789 490215**

PUBLISHED BY

DENNIS PUBLISHING LIMITED
Tel 020 7907 6000 **Fax** 020 7907 6020
FINANCE DIRECTOR **Brett Reynolds**
CHIEF EXECUTIVE **Alistair Ramsay**
CHAIRMAN **Felix Dennis**

Printed by Polestar Chantry

InsideEdge **is published monthly by Dennis Publishing Ltd, 30 Cleveland Street, London W1T 4JD, a company registered in England number 1138891.**

Entire contents © Dennis Publishing Ltd licensed by Felden. All email addresses are firstname_surname@dennis.co.uk

Join the poker revolution!

The most famous poker saying of them all has it that if you can't spot the sucker within the first half hour at the table, then *you* are the sucker.

If this saying wasn't true, it wouldn't have become so widespread and certainly wouldn't have been spoken by Matt Damon in the first few minutes of *Rounders* (1998), the best poker film ever made.

So it's the aim of this book to make sure that when you do sit down at a poker table, it's not you who will be identified as the sucker or 'fish' – the small-fry poker player whose bankroll is merely waiting to be devoured by the sharks sitting down with you.

The poker juggernaut

If you're new to poker, then the good news is that you've arrived at a great time. The world is seemingly in the grip of a poker craze, inspired by the online game. Fairytales such as those of Chris Moneymaker – who became the $2.5 million-winning World Champion after qualifying via a $40 satellite tournament on the internet – have inspired millions of people worldwide to log onto poker websites to start playing.

The game of poker is played in hundreds of variations, but the overview of the game contained in these pages concentrates mostly on Texas hold'em, as that's by far the most popular game played online and is the game played in the World Series of Poker main event, aka the Big One (the tournament won by Moneymaker in 2003 and Joseph Hachem this year in his first-ever appearance).

In order to play a decent game, you must learn the basic rules and procedures of poker, the values of the various combinations of cards, and basic strategies for betting. To that end, reading this book will give you a very good grounding.

The great leveller

Whatever anyone says, poker *is* a game of skill and there's a huge amount to learn if you want to play with the best.

But that's the egalitarian beauty of poker. There are no official hierarchies and no handicaps. You need no special equipment to play, only a few quid and a sizeable pair of (figurative) cojones. And although anyone can win on any given day, over the long haul, only the player with the most skill – an indefinable blend of wits, wiles, guts and guile – will leave the table clutching more money than they started with.

It's not often that you can test yourself against one of a game's greats. To tee up with Tiger Woods, for example, you have to be a fellow professional, a big-time celebrity or a wealthy captain of industry. If you get good at poker, though, you could well find yourself sitting at the same table in Las Vegas as the game's biggest stars – professional poker players such as Daniel Negreanu, Phil Hellmuth, David 'Devilfish' Ulliott or the 'Fossilman' himself, Greg Raymer.

The main thing, though, is to enjoy it – if it wasn't such fun, most people wouldn't bother playing it. Once you've read and understood this book, you'll appreciate that there's an adrenaline-pumping, mind-lasering buzz to poker. So get stuck into it now.

James Hipwell
Editor

EDITORIAL POLICY STATEMENT

Gambling could be harmful if not controlled and kept in moderation, and readers engage in such activity entirely at their own risk.

Dennis Publishing in no way encourages reckless gambling and it is recommended that readers who engage in gambling carefully monitor their activity and set financial limits. Anyone concerned about problem gambling can contact GamCare on 0845 6000 133 or *gamcare.org.uk* for further information.

While every effort is made to ensure the accuracy of editorial and advertising material in this publication, no claims for loss as a result of any errors will be accepted by the publishers. The opinions expressed herein are not necessarily those of the publishers themselves and are in no way intended to be relied upon.

Overseas-hosted websites are not regulated by UK legislation. Dennis Publishing can make no representation to readers of this publication as to the authenticity or conduct of the services advertised nor accept responsibility for activities relating to such sites.

This publication is not intended for persons under 18; it is illegal for such persons to engage in gambling (other than pool betting if aged 16 or over).

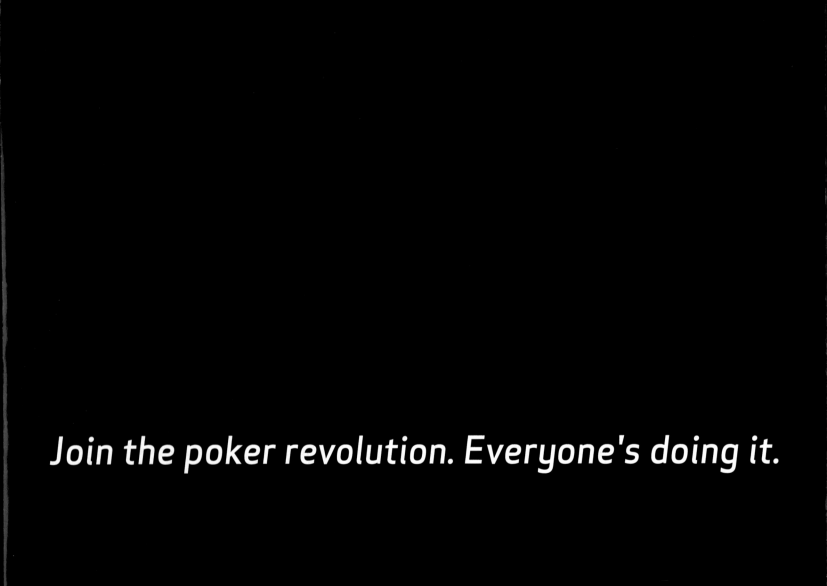

Join the poker revolution. Everyone's doing it.

32 year old IT consultant from Surrey. Has been a VC Poker player since June 2003, playing most days. Hobbies include swimming, going to good restaurants and watching TV (favourite programme is 24). A tight and careful player, he's the man to beat. Loves to play the odds, and mainly plays sit and go tournaments.

"Cool Hand Fluke"
AKA Luke Simmons

24 year old sales manager from London. Likes going to pubs, playing his games console and can't live without Sky+. Plays at VC Poker at least three times a week, and has a fast and loose style. His best moment came when he scooped enough in a multi-table tournament to take him and two mates to Amsterdam for the weekend.

"The Tooting Tiger"
AKA Josh Kennedy

32 year old events manager from Sussex. Life is ruled by the three S's: shopping, shoes and socialising. Introduced to poker by the guys at work, she's now the undisputed office champ. Almost impossible to bluff, her proudest moment was winning a satellite tournament to play in Las Vegas.

"The Lady Killer"
AKA Alison Churchill

26 year old graphic designer from Manchester. Loves clubbing and partying with friends, and fancies himself as a bit of a DJ. His massive record collection is his most treasured possession. When not hitting the clubs, he likes to mix it up on the $2/$4 No Limit tables. Proudest moment was getting paid off when hitting his first ever Royal Flush.

"Johnny Aces"
AKA John Lim

Contents

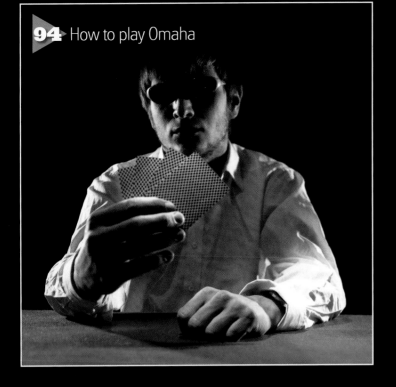

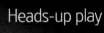

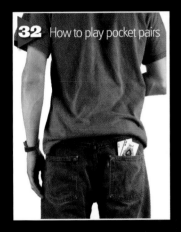

'Listen, here's the thing. If you can't spot the sucker in your first half-hour at the table, *you are* the sucker'

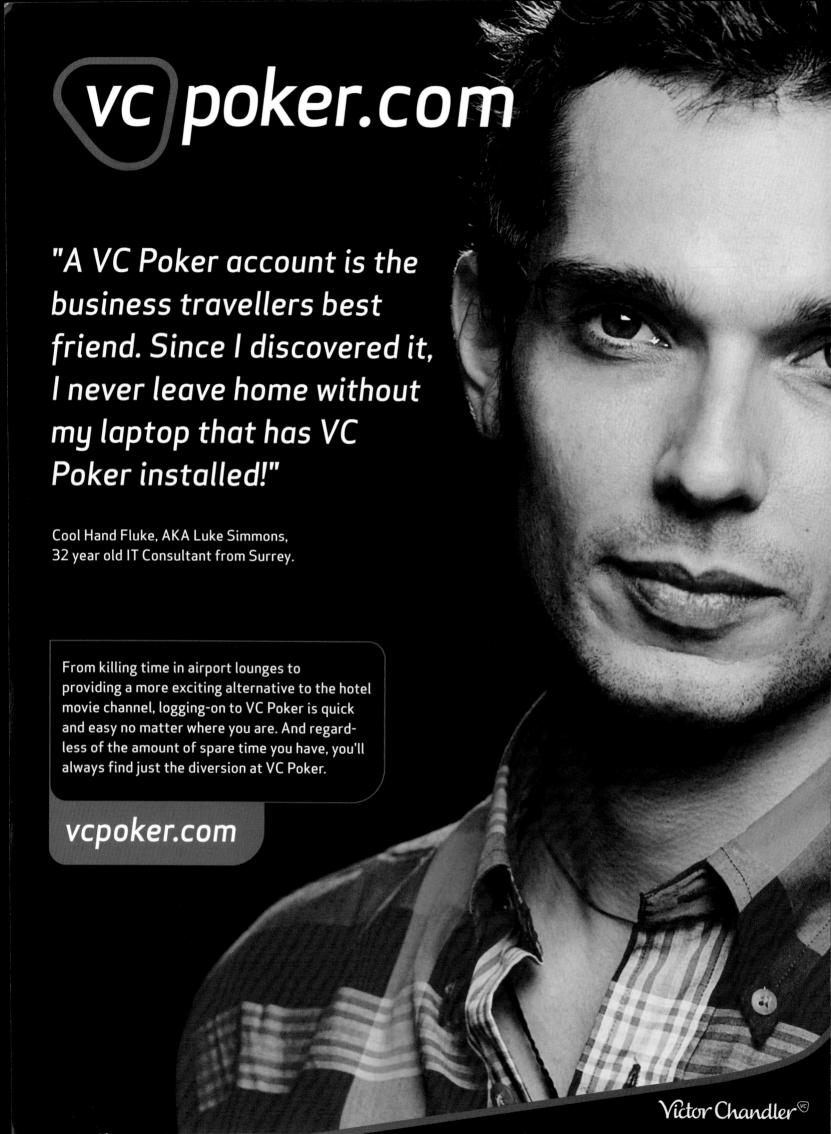

START ME UP!

Want to know how to play poker like the best of them and make yourself a nice profit into the bargain? You've come to the right place

Okay, so you're interested in playing poker and becoming more skilful at the game. However, before you start putting real money (or 'action' as you'll find it's called) on the table, there are a number of things to consider.

You have to know the hand ranks. Don't even go to the play-money tables online unless you're sure a straight beats three of a kind, a flush beats a straight and so on. You should also find out about the variants of the game – not just the difference between Texas hold'em and Omaha, but between limit hold'em, pot-limit hold'em and no-limit hold'em.

Thirty years ago, most poker players played seven-card stud, but hold'em has taken over as the dominant game in poker over the years, largely due to the high-profile World Series of Poker main event (which is a no-limit hold'em contest). As such, concentrate on hold'em at first.

Former world champion Doyle Brunson, who is known as the 'Godfather of Poker', says no-limit hold'em is the purest form of the game. He also wrote the most famous poker book of them all, *Super System*, and students of the game should certainly read this in their first year of play.

In this first section, we explain limit, pot-limit and no-limit hold'em, and give you basic strategies for playing them. At this early stage, one of the most important aspects of the game to learn about is which starting hands to play. One of our experts has devised a unique system based on the seasons for remembering which hands to play and which to pass. So if, after a few months, you're still playing J-8 suited 'under the gun' (that is, you're the first one to act in a hand), then leave the game and go back and read this section again.

Online play (on sites such as *vcpoker.com*) is usually in dollars, so it's this currency that features in the examples of online play used in this book. Remember, too, that before you commit your hard-earned cash to playing poker online, you can pit your wits against others on play-money tables. What have you got to lose?

Deal me in!
A beginner's guide to limit Texas hold'em

Want to learn poker but don't know where to start? Seen it on television or listened to your friends talking but afraid to give it a go? Then poker expert **Nolan Dalla's** guide to the easiest and cheapest format, limit Texas hold'em, will set you on the right path, taking you from internet 'play money' tables all the way to the big time

Sitting down to a poker game for the very first time can be a confusing, intimidating, even scary experience. I've played over half a million poker hands during my lifetime, and while I've forgotten playing almost all of them, the one hand that's still crystal clear is my first live poker hand dealt in a casino.

The year was 1983. Two months after my 21st birthday, I sat down in a $1/$4 seven-card stud game at the Flamingo Hilton in Las Vegas. The line-up at my table appeared mighty tough. The men with faces of stone looked like they'd been playing poker since World War II. The women, mostly grandmothers living on retirement cheques, were just as intimidating. I was the youngest player in the game by at least a quarter century. It was a textbook case of the Las Vegas locals (them) feasting on a tourist (me). Shark bait.

I anted up 25 cents. The exact cards that were dealt were irrelevant, but I recall how one of the chain-smoking old timers made it $4 to call, which was the maximum bet allowed at the table. I reached into my stack and, without any hesitation whatsoever, flung four dollar chips into the pot. They weren't going to push me around! I'd show them!

'Sir, don't splash the pot,' the dealer insisted. Splash the pot? What in the hell was he talking about? 'Sir, place

Before you even think of playing poker for real, an apprenticeship in online 'play money' poker should be mandatory

the chips in front if you intend to call, and I'll rake them into the pot,' the dealer instructed. Sure – I knew that. Right. 'No problem,' I said, hoping that my first infringement of poker etiquette would go unnoticed.

I might as well have fired off a flare gun. My opponent kept on betting on each round and by sixth street I'd seen enough. I folded, careful not to allow anyone to see my cards and the fact that I had no business in the hand in the first place. I'd played one hand of poker and was already stuck $17.25.

Around 30 minutes later, I was broke and stormed out, furious. Such was my first poker experience at a casino. What did I do wrong? Well, as you'll find out over the next few pages, just about everything. ➤

THE BASICS
A CRASH COURSE IN LIMIT TEXAS HOLD'EM

Clichéd but true: Texas hold'em is a deceptively simple game to learn, but a difficult game to master. It has surpassed all other forms of poker in popularity, leaving five-card draw, five-card stud, seven-card stud, and Omaha in the prairie dust. In fact, limit hold'em is spreading across Europe and the internet like wildfire. The basic rules are as follows...

Before the hand begins
The first thing to observe is the location of the dealer button, which means that player will act last on all betting rounds except the first. The player sitting to the immediate left of the dealer button is called the small blind. This player posts a small forced 'blind' bet in advance of the hand being dealt. In most limit hold'em games, this amount is one-half the size of the big blind.

The big blind sits to the immediate left of the small blind, and is exactly two seats to the left of the dealer. The big blind places a full-sized bet in advance. The remaining players do not ante, nor are they forced to place a bet before the deal begins. These players get to see a hand 'for free'. After each hand, the dealer button rotates one spot to the left, thus ensuring that every player plays one set of blinds during each orbit around the table.

How the cards are dealt
Each player is dealt two cards, both face down. These are called hole cards. They should never be disclosed to opponents, so make sure to protect your hand at all times. These are the only cards you will be dealt. Therefore, the most important decision you make in every hand is whether or not to play – which means either folding, calling, or raising.

The first round of betting
After you receive two hole cards, there is an initial round of betting. Now, you must decide if you want to play the hand. In limit hold'em, the size of the bet is always a fixed amount. This means betting increments on these early rounds are the same as the amount of the big blind. For example, if the big blind is 50¢, it will cost 50¢ to continue playing the hand.

The other options are to fold (which costs you nothing) or to raise. If you decide to raise, it must be exactly double the amount of the big blind. If there has already been a raise, and you have a very strong hand, you may want to re-raise. This means you will bet three times the size of the big blind.

If you are the small blind, you have the option of completing the bet to stay in the hand (costing you just one-half a bet if there's been no raise). If you're in the big blind, you're not required to place any more money into the pot on this round (unless someone has raised). Keep in mind that a good poker player does not bet or raise very often. The best players are patient and wait. They throw most of their weak hands away.

The flop
After the first round of betting, all of the chips are pooled in the centre of the table by the dealer. This is called the pot. Only players who still have hole cards compete for the pot. Next, the dealer turns three cards face up in the middle of the table. These three cards constitute the flop.

Now, you have a five-card poker hand – two hole cards and three flop cards. After the flop, there's another round of betting. The first active player to the left of the button will act, and the betting progresses around the table in a clockwise direction.

The turn
After the second round of betting, a fourth card is dealt and placed in the centre of the table. This is called the turn card (also known as 'fourth street'). The turn card means there are now six cards from which to make the best five-card poker hand. Now the stakes double in size from the previous round. For example, in a standard 50¢/$1 game, the initial bet on this round will be $1. Again, the active player to the left of the button is first to act, and the betting progresses around the table in a clockwise direction.

The river
After the third round of betting, a fifth card is dealt and placed in the centre of the table. This is the final card of the hand. This is called the river card (also known as 'fifth street'). The river card means there are now seven cards from which to make the best five-card poker hand. The betting stakes remain the same as the previous round. So, in a 50¢/$1 game, the betting amount on this round will be $1. Again, the active player to the left of the button is first to act, and the betting progresses around the table in a clockwise direction.

The showdown
After the final round of betting 'cards speak' – which means that the best five-card poker hand wins the pot. If you're in this long, you should be fairly confident you have the best hand at this point. Otherwise, why would you be in the hand?

the first hand I was dealt. And I went bust after half an hour. Be warned, and don't let this happen to you!

When you graduate from the 'play money' stakes you will start to find that people play a little differently. At the low and micro limits (you can play as small as 1¢/2¢ hold'em online) most might still be having fun, but as you get better and play bigger the opposition will take things more and more seriously. So if you want to join those among them aiming to make a profit from the game, big or small, you'd better start out right. Here's what I'd recommend for your game plan in your first 'real money' session:

● Take your seat and wait for the blinds (see The Basics box back on page 15) to come to you. Do not post a blind in advance. Wait patiently and watch the game.

● Make a commitment that the first hand you play will be very strong hand. Fold all hands which raise any doubt. This means that you will only play a big pair, or A-K. Throw everything else away.

● Since you should have already dedicated yourself to winning the first hand that you sit down to play and are following the strictest starting–hand guidelines, odds are that you should have the best hand when you finally do decide to play.

● If you lose that first hand for any reason, continue to practise the strictest starting-hand selection. Wait for a premium hand. Trust me – it will come. Eventually.

● If you are fortunate enough to win that first hand (not counting the blinds), go ahead and play more hands as you become more comfortable. Gradually, you will see what is

> Your first 'play money' game

When I first started playing poker, the internet didn't exist. If anyone wished to learn how to play poker in a casino, the beginner had to jump into the fire and get burned. But that's no longer the case. Now, with easy access to the net and multiple poker websites to choose from, it's much easier to learn the rules and nuances of poker for next to nothing.

Here's what you can do right now: download the free software at any of the major online poker sites – such as *vcpoker.com* – and play for fun. Since you're not playing for real money here, there's really no such thing as making a mistake.

Go ahead and try a few crazy things. With the click of a mouse, see what it's like to fold, call, bet, and raise. Watch the betting action and notice how the players are forced to act in turn. Notice that in 'limit' games, the bets conform to a certain size on each round of betting.

I strongly suggest that before you even think of playing poker for real, an apprenticeship in online 'play money' poker should be mandatory, however brief. There's really no better way to build up your poker confidence. Remember – when you play online, no one at your table knows who you are.

There's no reason to feel any pressure or be intimidated. Everyone was a beginner once. Furthermore, most players at the free-money tables will be beginners, and best of all, you can play online in the comfort of your own home without it costing a penny.

Your first 'real money' hand

Remember the story of my first poker hand? Back then, I didn't know the rules. I made the mistake of playing

▲ Trip Queens looks like a strong hand on the flop, but with possible draws still out there it would be best to bet strongly (or check-raise) and keep betting, unless it looks like someone has made their draw or has you beat

---

HOW A HAND UNFOLDS

You're holding a very playable A♥-K♥ for your two secret 'hole cards'. Do you fold, call or raise? Should you be jumping for joy or wetting your pants as the flop, turn and river come out? Let's see...

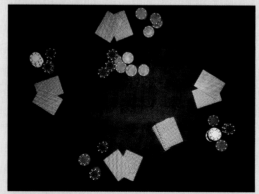

THE FIRST ROUND You are the player at the bottom of the picture. It's time to raise and get some money in this pot! A-K suited is almost the best you can hope for before the flop

THE FLOP With a flop of Q♥, A♠, J♥ you've got top pair, and a straight flush draw. Keep betting, or checkraise if you can – unless you think someone already has you beat

happening at the table and will be able to pick spots where you can play more hands, and even make some raises.
● Finally, don't be influenced by what you see from your opponents. Quite frequently they will show 'trash cards' and win big pots. Fact is, they got lucky. That happens in poker. But in the long run, players who play inferior cards, will lose. Count on it. Better yet, sit in their games. Love them. Just don't be one of them.

Hand selection – when to hold'em and when to fold'em

Imagine that two runners are to compete, and the first is given a significant advantage. Of course, that first runner would win a lot of the time. Why? Because he enjoyed an edge during the entire length of the race the other didn't have.

Now, let's think of this in poker terms. For example, if the first poker player begins with a powerful hand and plays an entire hand from start to finish against a second poker player who has a much weaker hand, which player will win most of the time? Naturally, the first player will win – in the long run.

This is why, obvious as it may sound. it's critical to start off each hand with good cards. In hold'em, the best starting hands are as follows: A-A, K-K, Q-Q, A-K (suited).

You should almost always play and raise (and re-raise) with these four powerhouse hands from any position. Unfortunately, these premium hands

> Needless to say, having any sort of gun to your head – metaphorical or otherwise – is not a particularly good position to be in

don't come very often – usually about once every 60 hands or so. You can also play the following hands, although they are not always worth making a raise: J-J, 10-10, 9-9, 8-8, 7-7, A-Q (suited), A-K (unsuited).

The remaining two-card starting hand combinations are open to question. Whether to fold, call, or raise with hands other than these listed depends on several factors, such as your position, the number of players already in the pot, and the type of game and the traits of the other players at your table.

Position – sitting on a goldmine or a time-bomb?

Most low-limit hold'em players and beginners fail to grasp the real importance of position at the poker table. Other than the two cards you are dealt, it's the single most important factor in your decision as to whether or not to play a hand.

In general, the later you act on each round of betting, the bigger your advantage. So, if you are the dealer, you enjoy the advantage of seeing what everyone else does before you.

Conversely, if you're in early position, you're at a distinct disadvantage. You must act first without knowing exactly how your opponent(s) will react.

So next we'll take a look at the impact of position in hold'em and what each category means to you:
● **The blinds** The small blind and big blind constitute the blinds. These two players are the first to act on each

▲ What a hand! You've beaten trip Aces, two pair, and a flush (plus the straight that came on the river) with your unbeatable straight flush on the turn! Who the hell shuffled this deck...?

round of post-flop betting. These players are in the worst possible position, since they have no idea what their opponents may have or do.

However, the blinds get to play more hands than other positions as they've already posted a bet and so will see many flops for free or one more bet.
● **Early position** The player to the immediate left of the big blind is called 'under the gun'. This player has a gun to his head, since he is the first player to decide whether or not to play the hand. Needless to say, having any sort of gun to your head – metaphorical or otherwise – is not a particularly good position to be in!

Both this player and the player on his left are considered to be in early position. It's recommended to play only the very best starting hands from early position in limit hold'em, such as A-A, K-K, Q-Q or A-K.
● **Middle position** In a full game of nine or ten players (which is fairly standard for most hold'em games), players who are fifth, sixth, and seventh in the betting rotation are considered to be in middle position. While players in middle position can play most of the hands listed earlier, they must also remember that there are at least three more players to act behind them.

Early position has very strict starting-hand guidelines and late position allows much more latitude, but how you play hands in middle position may be the single biggest determining factor when it comes to winning and losing in low-limit games. My advice is to play tight in this spot. Get more aggressive when you are sure you have the advantage, rather than trying to guess.
● **Late position** This normally refers to the last two or three players to act on each round of betting. In a ➤

THE TURN The 10♥ makes a royal flush, a hand rarer than a solar eclipse! It's too good to lead out with, unless you think other players won't bet. Lie in the bushes ready to pounce with a check-raise

THE RIVER The river doesn't change your unbeatable hand, but it makes a straight on the board, and now only a flush (or straight flush, ha, ha!) can win outright. Keep betting and pray for some action!

> ten-handed hold'em game, the eighth and ninth players in the rotation are in late position. These players enjoy an edge over players who act before them because they get the added benefit of knowing what the other players have done, before being forced to make a decision.

Players in late position are also less fearful of being raised, since most of the other players have already acted. Late position players are able to play a much wider range of starting hands (unless the pot has already been raised), including any pair, any suited Ace, any two face cards, and most suited connectors (hands such as 6-7 of the same suit, or 10-J of the same suit are playable in late position without a raise because they have both straight and flush potential).

● **Dealer** This is the strongest position in any hand. Even a 'bad' poker player enjoys some intrinsic advantages by virtue of his position at the table when he is the dealer.

In essence, this is much like being the last bidder at an auction. Imagine having the ability to know everyone's bid in advance before making your own. The dealer gets to see how every player acts on each round of betting and then can decide to fold, bet, raise, or re-raise. More bluffing is done from the dealer position than any other.

So there you have it – enough of an edge, we hope, to ensure you don't end up as shark bait the minute you test the water in the limit hold'em pond. But once you've caught the poker bug and have practised on the play money tables online, tested your nerve in live games, and generally become more confident about which hands are winning hands and how best to play them, you're going to want to raise your game to the next level. Make sure you're comfortable with all we've covered so far. Because you now have bigger fish to fry...

> **Even a 'bad' poker player enjoys some intrinsic advantages by virtue of his position at the table when he is the dealer**

TOP TIPS FOR TEXAS HOLD'EM

We've got yet more advice on improving limit hold'em play so you can take your opponents to the cleaners again and again!

Fold lousy hands!
It sounds so simple, doesn't it? Why, then, do so many players get involved in pots with bad cards? Many otherwise-decent players get attached to so-called 'trap' hands, which end up costing them a bundle. About ten years ago, I tracked every single poker hand I played for 18 straight months, and then tabulated my results. I found that I lost more money with J-K off-suit than any other hold'em hand. When I think of a lousy hand, I think of J-K.

In general, either raise or fold
This strategy works – try it. If you're not comfortable raising in many situations where you would normally just call, then why are you calling in the first place? Perhaps you shouldn't be in the hand if you aren't confident enough to make a raise. Obviously, there are exceptions to this guidance, such as calling with drawing hands in multi-way pots, but the 'raise or fold' strategy makes you an extremely troublesome person to play against, which is exactly what you should be trying to accomplish.

Respect kickers
In limit hold'em, more pots are lost at the showdown because of 'kicker trouble'

The evolution of (gambling) man

Just as evolution pertains to nature, becoming a winning poker player is normally a slow, arduous process. There's no way to turn a losing poker player into a winning poker player in a single day. There are no magic formulas or secret potions. Even if you read any of the highly acclaimed books on poker strategy currently out on the market, implementing their ideas takes time, not to mention hours and hours of practice.

Nevertheless, there are some fundamental precepts, which – if followed – can accelerate the evolutionary process from poker loser to poker winner. Elaborating on the basic concepts we've already covered, here are three quick tips for intermediate hold'em players that will instantly help your game:

● **Exercise better game selection** The most important decision you make when playing poker is the very first one – deciding in which game to play. This is most true for online poker, where the choice is unlimited. Finding the best possible game for your bankroll and comfort level should be your top priority, instead of 'getting to the action' as quickly as possible. All strategic decisions that follow derive from the far more meaningful initial decision as to whether or not the game is good versus bad. A skilful player playing against similarly skilful players will break even in the long run, while an average player playing against bad players will expect to turn a profit. So even though the skilful player in this example is better than the average player, his earning potential isn't as high due to poor game-selection practices. Oddly enough, I've seen poker players spend more time pondering what to eat at the dinner buffet than scouting the room and trying to find the best game. This, needless to say, is not the sign of a great poker player!

● **Make decisions based on the type of game you're in and the tendencies of your opponents, not your own mood or frame of mind** It's quite common to see players in mid-sized games come to the table with a certain mindset – for instance, to play tight, or be aggressive, or whatever their temperament happens to be for that session. Maximising earning potential requires that you first determine how others play and think, and then adapt to their style. Very tight games may demand more bluffing and aggression, whereas wild games might call for more simple, straightforward play. Essentially, you should always be flexible and adapt your style to the game at hand.

● **Recognise that as you move up in limit, position becomes much more important** In many small-stakes games, multiple callers routinely see every flop. This makes position less important than in games that are normally played with just a few players or heads-up after the flop. Acting last is a decisive advantage in mid-sized games because you gain the benefit of seeing

I've seen poker players spend more time pondering what to eat at a dinner buffet than scouting the room to find the best game

what actions your opponents take before you have to make a decision. By contrast, acting first in these more challenging games is always a disadvantage, as most skilled players constantly keep the pressure on opponents who are 'out of position'.

ADVANCED THOUGHTS

If you've made it up to the mid-sized games and you're a break-even player – congratulations. You might not realise it, but you're in the top 20% of poker players in this range. The fact that you managed to transform yourself from a losing to a break-even player shouldn't be taken too lightly. Think of it this way – if you're a break-even player, you obviously have developed some useful skills and are now in a position to advance even further.

As you advance, one of the things you must do is to 'think outside the box'. This means experimenting with different strategies beyond just the fundamental concepts, such as starting-hand selection, tight-aggressive play, and other proven winning methods normally applied to small-stakes games. Conventional play isn't good enough to beat most tougher games, so you have to go beyond a simple, straightforward approach. ➤

than any other clash of hands. This is especially true with Aces. An Ace with a small side-card is very tough to get away from when an Ace flops. If you bet and get called in any spot, you can't feel confident about your hand. Big cards with weak kickers are the proverbial ball and chain of limit hold'em. Unless you're in the blinds in an unraised pot, or you're

acting very late and might steal the blinds with a pre-flop raise, don't play high cards with weak kickers.

Blinds are a table toll, not an excuse to play more hands

If you were to calculate the wins and losses from every single seat you have played in your hold'em career, you would

have lost more money in the blinds than any other spot. Here's a hint: don't add to the losses. Blinds are the worst possible position, and against aggressive players, you're at a huge disadvantage. If you can't get in cheaply or re-raise with a strong hand, don't get involved. Calling liberally from the blinds should only be done in short-handed games and against very

weak-tight opponents who may be susceptible to a bluff after the flop.

Bluffing is vastly overrated, especially in limit games

Bluffing can be effective in tight games or against timid opponents. However, it should only be used selectively. Once you get tagged as a bluffer, you can't do much ➤

➤ One unconventional act is the notion of scrutinising your opponents. To be successful, you must try to get out of the box and into their heads, and try to pick up patterns, tells and tendencies so you can predict what an opponent might do in a given situation. In short-handed play, the cards sometimes don't matter, as the psychological battles between players can reach extreme levels.

For this reason, intimidation and table image are far more important in mid-sized games. Tough players who are winning chips are devastating opponents to play against. By contrast, bad players, no matter if they're winning or losing, are always good to play against and must be harvested.

Mid-sized hold'em games are the 'continental divide' of the poker world, economically speaking, as more players tend to play beyond their means. By comparison, small-stakes games rarely affect the financial status of the players in them. However, in a significant number of mid-sized games, people are playing near the edge of their economic means. This has dramatic consequences on the games in terms of the diversity of backgrounds, experiences, playing styles and skills of these players.

The survival of the fittest

As you move up, recognise that the skill differences between the players become increasingly minuscule. At the top levels, they're so small that most outsiders can't recognise them. For instance, there's a wide skill gap between the best and worst small-stakes players. At mid-sized games, these differences are less severe. In big games with skilled players, though,

table decisions are even closer (mathematically speaking) and more psychologically advanced. In the biggest games with the world-class elite, players ascend to a level of thinking that draws a fitting comparison to chess masters studying a board, always thinking several moves ahead.

Finally, if you're really determined to win the most amount of money possible by playing poker, be a positive

The world-class elite players tend to ascend to a level of thinking that draws a fitting comparison to chess masters studying a board

force in the games, even online where the social divide is most keenly felt. It's a good idea to make your opponents feel comfortable in your game – for example, by chatting. No one likes to lose money, but if your opponent has a bad night while also enjoying the game and playing with regular names, he's still likely to return. It's a wonderful paradox that players who are outclassed and are losing big will often remain in games for a long period as long as they're having a good time. Far too many pros forget this and lose out on potentially bigger earnings because they drive away inferior opponents with rude table manners. Sure, Darwin talked about the survival of the fittest, but don't forget that when we became civilised, we also worked out ways of making our livings without behaving like Neanderthals – so play poker like a gentleman, not a caveman! ❀

MORE TOP TIPS FOR TEXAS HOLD'EM

➤ more with it. One thing to consider is that players remember bluffers. We all recall when we were bluffed out of a big pot. You probably remember the person who bluffed you. You don't want to get tagged with this tactical albatross, because then you have to start playing 'showdown poker' (showing the best hand to win the pot), which means you

have effectively become card-dependent. Moreover, it's rarely wise to try to bluff more than one player, especially in limit games. (For more on bluffing techniques, see page 36.)

Be a 'zenmeister'

What's a 'zenmeister', you ask? Zen is a Buddhist philosophy that encourages

emotional tranquillity and acceptance of what has already transpired. Remember that bad beats happen to every single poker player. And, interestingly enough, bad beats happen more often to good players than to bad players. This is because the good players usually have the advantage – until doom falls, that is. The best poker

players learn to accept tough beats as part of the game. They recognise that losing control, or going 'on tilt', as it's otherwise known, causes more losses at middle-limit games than anything else. *Zen and the Art of Poker* by Larry W Phillips is an excellent read for all poker players who struggle to balance the bad times with the good.

Texas hold'em: no limit or pot limit?

Different playing styles and strategies are required for pot-limit and no-limit poker if you want to win big. **Phil Shaw** lays his cards on the table

No limit

If you want to play poker to any sort of level above that of 10¢-a-hand weekender, you need to know the differences between the pot-limit and no-limit versions of the game.

No limit is very exciting to watch, and easy to explain to new players. It does what it says on the tin: there is no limit to the amount you can raise. Pot limit is slightly more esoteric.

The maximum raise in pot limit is the total amount bet by all players, after you have matched the amount required to call. So if the blinds are $1 and $2 and nobody has bet yet, you can bet a maximum of $7 ($2 to call plus the total $5 on the table, made up of $3 blinds and your $2 call, which is counted as part of the pot).

There are several other important differences between pot-limit and no-limit poker, not least the context in which they are usually played. No-limit hold'em, variously referred to as 'the Cadillac of poker' and 'the crack cocaine of poker', owes its popularity almost solely to tournaments, the oldest and most prestigious of which is the $10,000 World Series Of Poker main event.

When hold'em was first played in the United States, no-limit cash games were common, but they dried up too quickly, as the top players soon took all the money. Basically, the pot-limit format was introduced to slow things down! Today, no-limit cash games are making a comeback on the internet, although pot limit remains popular both in tournaments and cash games, and is often preferred by more experienced players.

If you're playing either pot limit or no limit in a cash game or at the start of a tournament, there is no reason for hasty action, as the blinds are low in relation to the total number of chips in play. You need to be playing mainly either hands that are very strong – like A-A, K-K, A-K and Q-Q – or hands that can catch out less well-advised players, like small pairs that draw to three of a kind, and suited connectors (7♣-8♣ for instance) that draw to straights and flushes.

Just how big the big hands need to be depends on the level of game you play in. In a small game, other players may not even understand the importance of kickers, giving you a big advantage. In contrast, in the first few hours of the WSOP $10,000 main event, the blinds start so small and the skill level is so high that many players would only risk all their chips pre-flop with pocket Aces.

If you've got a strong hand, use it!

The classic beginner's mistake in big-bet games is to play strong hands too weakly before the flop, then put all the money in on the next (more expensive) rounds after someone else has made a better hand. Aces is the prime example here, as K-K and Q-Q can look weak when an overcard such as an Ace flops. Some players seem to think A-A is invincible, whereas it's often a one-way ticket to a disappointingly small win or a murderously big loss.

Pairs generally play strongly providing no overcards or obvious draws come on the flop (eg if you have Q-Q on a broken flop of 2♣, 5♥, 10♦), but you will need to bear in mind that anyone with a smaller pair has a 15/2 chance of hitting three of a kind, and since poker is based on such odds, you need to try and ensure you are not giving others an incentive to draw out on you. The way to do this is to raise by a sizeable amount in the first place.

In no limit, you can bet what you want, so the standard raise of three times the big blind or the pot could be a disaster if the blinds are still small and you run into the above situation against 2-2, 5-5 or 10-10. To avoid this, you might bet 10-15% of your chips, or more. Maximise the action and minimise the risk.

Pot limit, by contrast, is still in many ways a drawing game where raises are restricted. So if the blinds are small, you might not be able to raise enough to protect A-A or K-K. In this instance, good players sometimes go for a check-raise in order to get more chips in, and play big hands slowly if they can't get a lot of money in pre-flop.

> **No-limit hold'em has been variously described as 'the Cadillac of poker' and 'the crack cocaine of poker'**

The other strong hands in big-bet hold'em are of the A-K and A-Q variety. In tough games, A-Q has been called a trouble hand as strong, tight players only play or represent the very big pairs and A-K if they are not drawing, but if playing in loose, low-stakes, high-blind or late-position situations, it is playable, as are A-J, A-10, K-Q and K-J.

As with big pairs, you should raise enough in no limit to shut out draws if you feel your hand is initially the best. ➤

Pot limit

DECISIONS
SOME EXAMPLES OF HOW TO BET IN EACH FORMAT

CASH
Your hand A-K (suited) Game style Any Position Middle Blinds Any

What do you do?
One player limps (flat calls), you make a raise and both the blinds and the limper call. The flop comes down A♠, K♥, 6♥, and again you bet after the limper checks. Now the small blind calls, the big blind raises and the initial limper re-raises! What do you do?

A lot depends on your opinions of the other players, and how wild they are. Considering this as a possible deep-stack, casino, pot-limit game hand and a short-stacked, online, no-limit hand throws up divergent possibilities.

Pot limit
Against good opposition, you might actually have to throw your hand away. The most likely hand for the limper is 6-6 as he called then called again after you made a raise that was restricted to the size of the pot and two others came in. That player would then naturally check the flop, letting someone else bet the A or K and re-raising for a massive amount!

It's likely the small blind has a weaker hand, as in late position he would raise with something very strong to protect the hand, and the big blind could have started with almost anything as he already has money invested, cannot be raised out and was getting very good odds to catch a well disguised hand. The fact that he called could mean he has something along the lines of A-x of hearts.

No limit
In a short-stacked, no-limit game, the format and mobility of your stack means you can raise 10-15% pre-flop should you wish to, and should you think other loose players will call. In such a game you would hope to give a hand like 6-6 bad odds to call, so even if this loose player catches you here in the long term they will lose it back calling with small pairs that miss.

People may well play hands like weak Aces stronger than is advisable in this situation, and could call with any kind of flush draw. So in a wild, short-stacked, no-limit game, you would often raise all-in to block out draws as far as possible and snare the second-best hands, especially if the limper is a maniac or one of the blinds raises instead of him. Even if you end up losing, you have protected your hand well pre-flop and if the other players are so loose and indiscriminate as to put money in with inferior hands, you could end up the winner in the long term.

TOURNAMENT
Your hand A-A Game style Loose Position First Blinds 25 and 50

What do you do?
Here, the format is of less importance. Your primary concern is how the players behind you are going to respond to your play.

Pot limit
If you check and nobody raises you, the Aces are in serious jeopardy as you have let draws in and you can still only bet the pot. If you check-raise successfully, you may force players to fold, and also make them play more cautiously in future. However, if you bet the pot you are still letting people call with drawing hands for a reasonable sum, and if the maniacs only call, it's likely more people will come in as the action moves round the table as there are so many chips on offer.

No limit
Here, you face similar problems to the same scenario in pot limit, but if you can make a big raise of say 250-400, you may shut out any draws and suck in the players who call big raises. However, you risk everyone folding.

The answer here is not so much to do with the betting format as with how you play the Aces. You should play them in the same manner as other hands in order not to arouse suspicion. Pot limit is great for this, as making a pot-sized raise can mean a wide variety of hands. In no limit, you will need to be careful to bet similar amounts most of the time so as not to give the strength of your cards away. Remember that if you have bet out strongly pre-flop, you can keep betting strongly afterwards, but if you try for a check-raise and fail, you will need to proceed with caution!

➤ In pot limit, you must bear in mind the ratio of a pot-sized raise to your stack size, so you don't lose a lot of money to a draw. A-K needs to connect with an A or K on the flop to be bet strongly, but you can still bluff if you think the other players are weak, tight or respect you for strong hands.

As the blinds go up in tournaments, the value of the weaker Aces and face cards rise and the value of drawing hands fall, so with few bets left, A-Q and A-J are certainly hands you can raise or move all-in with, as are big and medium pairs. The key here is that with weaker hands you want to be the one raising to steal the blinds and make others fold, and you want to do this before anyone else has made a bet. When raising in the late stages of a pot-limit tournament with a medium hand, you also need to be aware of how much of your stack you can get in the middle in one go.

Show me the money

In pot-limit and no-limit cash games, since the blinds stay the same, money is only usually going to change hands when players make mistakes. Cash games can be played pot limit (favoured in casinos) or no limit (favoured online) and can be played with a lot of money on the table (casinos) in relation to the size of the blinds or relatively little (online). You need to adapt to the style of game you are playing in.

Deep-stack, pot-limit games naturally tend to attract skilful players eager to exploit the innocents who raise the pot to $7 from their $200 stack with Aces before the flop and proceed to put in the other $193 on the next rounds when they have fallen

The early-round restriction on betting in pot limit makes it a more draw-based game. In no limit you can usually bet a draw out of existence

behind to a pair that made trips, or are in considerable danger from a number of draws.

No-limit games tend to be wilder and more volatile, with people raising and moving in frequently, which gives more opportunities to make quick money from bad players, but also removes the constraints that usually allow you to draw hands in.

The standard of the game also has a massive bearing on the quality of hands you need to win big pots. For example, in a fast, loose, no-limit game you might tempt a short-stacked, inexperienced player to move all-in with a weak Ace against your A-K before the flop, whereas in a skilful, deep-stacked game it is common to only see money changing hands because of a powerful bluff and/or excellent call, or a clash of massive hands such as two players both making a full house.

The key to both pot-limit and no-limit hold'em is rooted in understanding the other players, the odds and how the amounts on the table relate to what you can bet at any given stage. The principal difference you should remember is the restriction on betting in the early rounds in pot limit, making it a more draw-based game, whereas in no limit you are usually in a position to bet a draw out of existence.

To be a successful player, you should really try both formats. By playing pot limit you will learn the importance of drawing hands, which can, in turn, help you learn how to protect a big hand in no limit. Both games require a lot of skill and self control because any decision can be extremely costly. If you can become a strong, disciplined player there are limitless amounts of money out there to be won. ❀

KNOW WHAT YOU'RE TALKING ABOUT
POKER BETTING TERMINOLOGY

TEXAS HOLD'EM

A poker game where each player receives two cards face down and must then make the best five-card hand using them and/or the five community cards, which everyone uses. Betting occurs after each of four rounds of dealing:

1 **'Hole' cards** – a player's two hidden cards, that only they know and can use.
2 **The flop** – the first three community cards, dealt in one go.
3 **The turn** – the fourth community card.
4 **The river** – the final community card.

The winner is the last person with hole cards (ie if the final bet is unmatched as all other players have folded) or the person with the best five-card hand according to the ranking of poker hands.

POT LIMIT/NO LIMIT

In pot limit, a player can bet anything up to the exact amount in the pot and in no limit they can bet anything up to their total number of chips. Beginners should also note that you can 'check', meaning to not bet, providing nobody else has already bet on that round, and call, meaning to match the previous bet but not raise or fold.

TABLE STAKES

The rule, almost universally applied in modern poker games, whereby a player cannot be bet off the table. If a bet exceeds the amount a player has, they are simply declared 'all-in' and entitled to see the hand to the end and win from each other player an amount up to or matching what they have put in.

BLINDS

Compulsory bets that get the action going. In poker, the cards are dealt and decisions are made in a clockwise path from the dealer button. The person to the left of the dealer button posts the small blind and the next person the big blind (usually double the value of the small blind). These blinds determine the size of the game and create the action as there is always something in a hand for players to compete for. On the first round, the person after the big blind acts first; in all subsequent rounds the person to the left of the button is first to act. In a cash game the blinds remain fixed, but in a tournament they are raised according to a predetermined structure to ensure that the tournament plays down to one player.

Frosty Outlook

3 ♥

5 ♣

LOW

Dangerous Conditions

Slippery

WEATHER TO PLAY OR TO PASS

Knowing whether to play or pass a hand is one of the most important aspects of Texas hold'em. **Professor Leighton Vaughan Williams** introduces his own innovative 'calendar' hand-grouping strategy and forecasts that using it will help you to rake in those monster pots all year round

Playing poker is fun, but so are a lot of other things in life. What makes poker special is that you can win money at the same time. Poker also possesses the same sort of mystical attraction that draws so many to tank driving – the idea of going to war sitting down!

Well, that's the theory. In reality, of course, it's just not that easy. As any tank driver can tell you, the best laid plans can easily go awry in the fog of battle. Similarly, you can know all you like about the odds and sods of poker statistics, but any seasoned player can tell you that theory can take you only so far in the real hurly-burly of live competition.

What's just as critical is an understanding of what's important, being able to utilise that understanding, and being able to make the right decisions even when under pressure, time and time again.

I'm not saying that an understanding of the finer details of poker probability theory isn't a real advantage when it undeniably *is*. But what I am saying is that a long-term winning strategy requires more than a little of 'something else'. Indeed, I have come to believe that this particular

element is actually a lot more important than either a ready acquaintance with almanacs of poker probabilities or access to streams of statistical software. In this article, I'll introduce you to one such 'something else' – a certain something which I've named 'calendar' strategy. You'll soon see why.

The heat of the moment

The first key idea is to determine what's really important to a winning poker strategy, and the second is to formulate this in a way which can actually be turned into a practical strategy. The method I will outline below is in fact based on a lot of statistical analysis, only it's presented in a way which can be of best use to those without the slightest interest in statistics or probabilities but who do have a significant interest in playing winning poker.

It's meant to serve as an alternative to the conventional approaches to pre-flop strategy available in most books on this subject, which, in general, make what should be a relatively simple ➤

> **Poker possesses the same sort of mystical attraction that draws so many to tank driving – the idea of going to war sitting down**

Sunny Outlook

What a Scorcher!

HIGH

> decision seem very complicated indeed, with advice that's extremely difficult to retain or recall, let alone understand in the first place. My system is simpler and more accessible.

As you know, in Texas hold'em each player is dealt two cards and must make a decision whether to fold the cards without playing, to call someone else's bet or to raise the bet. Because this decision has to be made before any other cards are dealt, the key issue is gauging the likely strength of your hand compared to your opponents' hands.

The problem, of course, is that you have no idea what cards your opponents are holding, other than the fact that they can't be holding exactly the same cards as you. What you can know, however, is that a particular hand is generally worth playing more strongly than another. For example, if experience suggests that raising with an Ace and a Queen of the same suit (A-Q suited) is a good strategy, what should you do if you're handed a pair of tens? If calling with a pair of sixes late in the betting round is a good strategy, what does that tell you if you're last to play and are looking down at a J-10 off-suit?

Strength in numbers

Indeed, an understanding of the pecking order of possible hands is the foundation of basic strategy. With the benefit of this understanding and based also on your table position and previous calls and/or raises, it's possible to devise a ground-plan for playing the game.

> **You have to be able to access this information and the core strategy derived from it under pressure in real time**

First, however, you need to be confident in the order of strength of pre-flop hands, and second, you have to be able to access this information and the core strategy derived from it under pressure in real time. Which is where my calendar strategy comes in – it's designed so you can apply it before the flop whatever your hand is.

It works like this. The system ranks each possible pre-flop hand, and selects 52 as playable in normal circumstances, depending on where you are seated relative to the dealer and who has played what before your turn comes. The best hands are called January hands, the worst playable hands are called December hands. The first week of January corresponds to the strongest hand possible – a pair of Aces, the second week to the second strongest hand – a pair of Kings, and so on.

An unorthodox approach

Any hands not on the calendar at all should probably be folded. There may be exceptions, if you're a particularly adventurous or experienced player, where there may be a case for occasionally playing off-calendar, as I term it. Really, though, this is the poker equivalent of skiing off-piste – only for the bold, the ultra confident and those who really know what they're doing.

Because there are 12 months in a year, but 52 weeks, some months are allocated five weeks for these purposes and some four. Months of cards are then grouped into seasons – January, February, March and April cards are known (somewhat optimistically) as spring cards, and

SPRING HANDS (played in all positions)

JANUARY	FEBRUARY	MARCH	APRIL
A-A	10-10	A-10 (suited)	K-10 (suited)
K-K	A-Q (suited)	K-J (suited)	8-8
Q-Q	A-J (suited)	A-Q (off-suit)	Q-10 (suited)
J-J	A-K (off-suit)	9-9	A-9 (suited)
A-K (suited)	K-Q (suited)	Q-J (suited)	A-J (off-suit)

SUMMER HANDS (played in middle/late positions)

MAY	JUNE	JULY	AUGUST
J-10 (suited)	10-9 (suited)	A-7 (suited)	A-3 (suited)
K-Q (off-suit)	9-8 (suited)	A-6 (suited)	A-2 (suited)
7-7	8-7 (suited)	A-5 (suited)	K-J (off-suit)
J-9 (suited)	A-8 (suited)	A-4 (suited)	Q-J (off-suit)

AUTUMN HANDS (played in late position)

SEPTEMBER	OCTOBER	NOVEMBER	DECEMBER
J-10 (off-suit)	3-3	Q-10 (off-suit)	6-5 (suited)
6-6	2-2	K-9 (suited)	5-4 (suited)
5-5	A-10 (off-suit)	J-8 (suited)	4-3 (suited)
4-4	K-10 (off-suit)	7-6 (suited)	3-2 (suited)

OFF-CALENDAR Stronger (ie less weak) hands

10-8 (suited)	K-2 (suited)	K-3 (suited)	Q-5 (suited)
9-7 (suited)	K-8 (suited)	Q-3 (suited)	Q-4 (suited)
8-6 (suited)	K-7 (suited)	Q-9 (suited)	Q-2 (suited)
7-5 (suited)	K-6 (suited)	Q-8 (suited)	
6-4 (suited)	K-5 (suited)	Q-7 (suited)	
5-3 (suited)	K-4 (suited)	Q-6 (suited)	

Once you have mastered the calendar, the next step is to learn the optimal plays for hands associated with the different times of year, ie whether to raise, call or fold when your turn comes to play. As a guide, I suggest the following, but you can, of course, revise and adapt based on your own playing experience and your knowledge and intuition about your opponents as you become more familiar with the system. You should always err more on the side of caution the later in the month or the season the hand falls.

SPRING CARDS

JANUARY Raise (even if raised) in all positions
FEBRUARY Raise (call if already raised) in all positions
MARCH Call in early position, raise (call if already raised) in middle or late position
APRIL Call in early or middle position, raise (call if already raised) in late position

SUMMER CARDS

MAY, JUNE, JULY, AUGUST Call in middle or late position (fold if already raised)

AUTUMN CARDS

SEPTEMBER, OCTOBER, NOVEMBER, DECEMBER Call in late position (Fold if already raised)

More generally, the looser you consider the game (ie the weaker the hands you think your opponents are playing), the later in the calendar you might consider playing instead of folding. Beware, however, of players preceding you who have indicated strength by raising.

Ultimately, of course, there's no definitive system for playing your hand in a game of Texas hold'em poker. If there was, we'd all be winning millions in the World Series of Poker, and there'd be no call for books like this one. There are, however, better and worse strategies, and a convenient way to access the relative strength of hands is important in determining which is which. Poker should be fun. If the 'calendar' system adds to the fun, I'll be pleased. If it helps you win – and it's not off *me* – I'll be delighted! ✾

should be considered in early position and later. May, June, July and August cards are known as summer cards, and should be considered in middle position and later, while September, October, November and December cards are autumn cards, and should be considered in late position only.

A guide to position in a ten-handed game is to consider late position as the dealer button and one seat to the right of that, the next three seats to the right as middle position, and the next three to the right as early position. This can, of course, quite easily be adapted for games with fewer players.

Let me check my diary...

To summarise the general principle, the best hand, a pair of Aces (A-A), is the first week of January while, conversely, the weakest playable hand, a three and a two of the same suit (3-2 suited), represents the last week of December. January's cards are: A-A, K-K, Q-Q, J-J, A-K (suited) while December's are: 6-5 (suited), 5-4 (suited), 4-3 (suited), 3-2 (suited). Whether you call or raise or re-raise depends also on how early/late in the season your cards fall.

The big advantage of this calendar system is that most people should find it a fairly easy way to memorise the relative strength of hands, and how to play them. Just as importantly, though, it uses what is, in my view, the best available analysis to work out which hands are superior to which. Utilising this analysis can be a great help when it comes to honing your skills at the table. You should start by familiarising yourself with the complete calendar, shown in the next column.

WHY CHOOSE VC POKER?

1 You can practise your game on the play-money tables. Learn at your own pace, on your own terms.

2 With a huge choice of real-money tables, you won't have to hang around for hours waiting to get a game.

3 There's a wide range of table stakes to suit all players. Watch and learn as high-rollers drop fortunes. Watch and laugh as your mates play at stakes well beneath your interest. Discover the right level for you and work your way up.

4 VC Poker offers one of the largest selections of tournaments anywhere on the web, with buy-ins ranging from 10¢ to $500.

5 Because you're dealing directly with VC Poker, you can always play safe in the knowledge that you're in a 100% fair and secure environment.

6 The state-of-the-art yet cunningly simple software means you don't need to be a rocket scientist to play on the site. Download it now and see what we mean. Turn off the lights and it's just like having a poker room in your house.

7 VC Poker offers unparalleled 24/7 customer service to support you whenever you need it. Phone for help if you encounter any difficulties at all. Someone's always on hand to talk you through the problem – or to listen to your bad beat stories.

8 More than just poker software, VC Poker is a poker community that brings together tens of thousands of poker enthusiasts from all over the world. Take advantage of it and get stuck in.

9 There are lots of great promotions, offers and competitions to motivate, inspire and challenge you.

10 With thousands of registered players, you'll always be able to get a game. So what are you waiting for?

GETTING STARTED ONLINE

So you want to get in on the action? Well, it has never been easier, with our step-by-step guide to getting your computer ready to play VC Poker online

So you wanna play poker, and you wanna play right now? You've come to the right place. Downloading and installing the VC Poker software is a piece of cake. To get going, just go to *vcpoker.com*, click on 'Download Now' and select 'Open' when the dialog appears.

If you have any difficulty, or would just like a real person to talk you through the process, get in touch with the VC Poker support team, who'll be happy to give you a helping hand.

Step one
Download the poker client
Getting started at VC Poker is a quick, easy and straightforward process. However, before you do anything, you have to get the poker room client, which is just a technical way of saying that you need to download the software that connects to the VC Poker servers. Once you've done this, you're ready to install the software.

Step two
Install the poker client
The next step is installing the poker client on your PC. The good news is that it does all the hard work for you. Simply double-click on the icon and the software will self-install. As the client completes its installation, it will connect with the poker room and show you a registration window.

Step three
Register with us
Once you've connected to the poker room, you'll see the lobby area. You can check out a few games without registering. However, if you'd like to start playing, you'll need to register, which doesn't take long. You'll need to choose a unique screen name, password and avatar, and also supply a little more information about yourself. Choose something you're happy with, as you won't be able to change it afterwards.

Step four
Open a real-money account
Play money is fun, but, let's face it, winning $100 of real chips is much better. If you want to play for real money, you need to open an account with Victor Chandler. To do this, select 'Cashier' from the lobby. If you want to enter any freerolls, you need to go through this process. Should you win, you need somewhere to put your winnings. You can use switch, visa and so on to deposit money in seconds, and also to withdraw your cards. All play is in US dollars, and there are fixed exchange-rates for deposits and withdrawals.

Step five
Sit back, play poker and enjoy
That's it, you're now ready to dive straight into the world of online poker. Have fun, and good luck!

> **Play money is fun, but, let's face it, winning $100 of real chips is much better**

vc poker.com

"The psychology, the sheer courage of making of play, winning big, talking in slang, the crazy nicknames. Man, there's no game on earth as cool as poker."

Johnny Aces AKA John Lim, 26 year old graphic designer from Manchester.

Played by millions of real people from all over the world, poker is the world's coolest game. And if you'd like to see what all the fuss about, VC Poker offers a safe, fun and friendly place to discover why the world's gone mad for online poker.

vcpoker.com

Victor Chandler

BACK TO SKILL

Your game's improving, you're well on your way to becoming a poker pro. However, you won't get very far if you don't take the time to brush up on the requisite skills and strategy...

You now know about the variants of Texas hold'em and have gleaned some knowledge about which hands to play and which to pass, as well the importance of position. That's great, but it isn't going to win you a coveted World Series of Poker bracelet.

Now it's time to develop your poker skills and learn the strategies that will give you a shot at the big time. There are many examples of relative novices, people who have only been playing poker for a year, going to Vegas and competing with the best in the world in some of the richest tournaments on the gambling calendar.

In this section, we cover strategies for playing pocket pairs. What should you do if you look at your cards and see that you've been dealt a pair of 9s, or even Aces (also known as Pocket Rockets or American Airlines)?

You'll also learn about the importance of bluffing, when to do it and how not to get caught with your metaphorical trousers down. A good bluffer sees when his opponent has a weak hand and instinctively knows how to exploit the situation with a bluff. This kind of information can make the difference between winning and losing at poker in the long term.

Something else that will help you to win is realising that every poker player has what are called 'tells' – that is, they give off unconscious indications of the strength or weakness of their hand. In this section, we teach you what to look for in an opponent that might cause them to give their game away. You'll be amazed at how universal the tell is: one top pro, who shall remain nameless, always gives the table some banter if he has a weak hand, but is hit by a stony silence if he has a good hand.

Finally, you'll also read about one of the most important elements of the game in this section: calculating pot odds. If you go into a large pot without knowing whether you're getting good odds (or value), you won't be able to progress much in the poker, so learn the odds and learn them well!

IS THAT A PAIR IN YOUR POCKET?

... Or are you just pleased to see us? From deuces to pocket rockets, poker expert **Andrew NS Glazer** has the best playing strategies for every pair in Texas hold'em

Pocket pairs are potentially some of the most profitable hands in hold'em, but because they are so often misplayed – usually overplayed, sometimes underplayed – they don't add as much to your day's win or your tournament chances as they should.

I'm going to examine the nature of pocket pairs here, focusing primarily on their use in no-limit tournaments. I'll also offer notes for low-limit money players too, though, so don't run away if you only play small-limit or pot-limit games. Every hold'em player will learn something useful.

Let's start with 'The Worst Play In Poker'. I'm astounded by the number of players who get this one wrong. It's calling an all-in bet with a small pair.

If you call all-in rather than betting or raising all-in, you only have one way to win: holding the best hand. It's far better to have two ways to win when you make a bet; either with your bet, or with your hand. Suppose you knew that your hand was a 3/2 underdog to win – that you only had a 40% winning chance. Suppose further that you knew that if you bet all-in, your opponent would fold 50% of the time.

It would be correct to bet, even though you knew you had the inferior hand. In 100 confrontations, you would win 50 without a fight, and of the other 50, you would win 20. You wind up winning 70 of the 100 confrontations. While you can't know the odds this precisely at the table, this example shows how having two ways to win often easily turns an inferior hand into a winner.

However, if you call all-in, you're going to find yourself in one of two situations: either you'll be roughly even money (against two overcards), or you'll be roughly a 9/2 underdog (small pair against larger pair).

Do you really want to put all your chips into the pot when it's impossible for your opponent to fold and you're either a small favourite or a huge underdog? It's a ridiculous play if you look at it realistically, and yet you'll see players again and again make huge calls with hands like pocket 4s.

The 'coin flip' myth

Whenever you watch televised poker and you see someone with a pocket pair going up against someone with two overcards (such as Q-Q vs A-K or 7-7 vs 8-9), you almost always hear the announcers say one of two things: either the hand is a 'coin flip,' (meaning

It's best to have two ways to win: either with your bet or with your hand. But if you call all-in, you can only win with your hand

that it's a 50/50 chance) or that 'it's roughly 11/10 in favour of the pair.' Listen for it: it's practically universal.

The only problem is, it's practically universally wrong. Different pocket pairs are different sized favourites against different overcards. In fact, they aren't always favourites. J-10 suited is a favourite over every single pair from twos through sevens, if the pair doesn't contain one of the suited cards, and usually even if it does. You need to reach pocket eights before the pair becomes the favourite, and that's by a tiny amount.

On the other hand, if you take your pocket sevens – or even your pocket deuces, for that matter – up against A-K, you're the favourite. Can you guess why the J-10 hands do so well? **There are four main ways in which overcards can defeat a pocket pair:**
● To hit one (or more) of the overcards. For example, Q-Q vs A-K, and the final board is 5, K, 7, J, 2.
● To make a straight (a single card from a pair can also help make a straight, but two connected cards stand a much better chance). For example, 7-7 vs J-10, with the final board coming 8, 9, Q, 7, 2 (notice that even making a set of 7s on the turn didn't save the pocket pair).
● To make a flush (very similar to the straight analysis). For example, 8♥-8♥ vs Q♠-J♠ with the final board coming 10♠, 9♠, A♥, 3♥, 8♠. Notice the same river card that gave the eights their 'lucky' set also created the flush: remember such possibilities when calculating 'outs' (winning cards).
● To get counterfeited – one of the biggest problems with tiddly pairs. For example, 3-3 vs A-9, and the final board comes 5, 5, 6, 10, 6. The owner of the 3s must play the board, while the opponent can use his Ace. Any time you own a small pair and a larger pair flops, be careful.

Because J-10 makes more high straights than any other hand, if you owned a pair of fours, you would actually much prefer to be up against the powerful looking A-K, which makes far fewer straights, than against J-10.

If you own Q-Q and are up against A-K, you are lucky enough to be in the single most favourable 'pair vs overcards' situation. Express it however you like: 4/3, or 1.33/1, or a 57.2%; no matter which way you describe it, you are quite far away from coin-flip territory.

You own this significant edge because your two Queens reduce the A-K's chances of winning with a straight. A-K's owner will need a queen to hit the board to make a straight, and you have two of them tucked safely away. Don't get too excited by this information, though. Many players, upon learning that J-10 makes more straights than any other hand start to rank J-10 far too highly.

Smaller pairs
I split pocket pairs into several distinct value groups. Let's start at the bottom and work our way up:
● Small pairs (2-2, 3-3, 4-4, and 5-5). Although these hands stand a reasonably good chance of winning a heads-up confrontation against overcards, they have several major vulnerabilities. In a game where three or more players see the flop, they usually need to make a set to win. Small pairs are also the most vulnerable to getting counterfeited. The good news is that their unimproved post-flop weakness is so obvious that even bad players are usually willing to throw them away, something that can't always be said of...
● Middle pairs (6-6, 7-7, and 8-8). For the most part, these hands play like small pairs. The biggest difference is that they don't get counterfeited nearly as often, and occasionally in heads-up confrontations you will find yourself facing only one overcard instead of two. Otherwise, these hands can be more troublesome than small pairs, especially if the board comes low – 10, 4, 2, for instance. A player holding pocket eights will often think 'only one overcard hit, I might be leading,' and bet aggressively, not realising he is up against someone who has that one overcard or someone who is tentatively calling with a hand like 9-9. Normally, unless you flop a set or a good straight draw (that is, the board is 4, 5, 6 and you have 7-7), you should get out.
● Danger pairs (9-9, 10-10). These are much like middle pairs, but occasionally will hold up against an opponent who has hit part of his hand (like, for example, someone playing A-8 suited who hits the 8). They should be played like middle pairs, but you will very rarely get counterfeited. I call them danger pairs because players tend to push them too hard. Beware and don't make the same mistake. ➤

vc poker.com

"I can honestly say that I've made real friends through VC Poker. I never expected online poker to be so social, but playing and chatting with people is really fun."

The Tooting Tiger AKA Josh Kennedy, 24 year old sales manager from London.

VC Poker is more than just a poker room, it's a poker community. With tens of thousands of real people logging-on every day, dive right in and play and chat with real people in the web's friendliest poker room.

vcpoker.com

There's a poker player inside everyone.
Let yours out @ www.vcpoker.com

Victor Chandler VC

➤ Royal couples

● J-J: The single trickiest hand in no-limit. It wins just enough without improvement to give its owner confidence, yet is extremely vulnerable in multi-way situations. If you are facing all three overcards, you are a significant underdog. Just how big varies: you're far better off being up against A-K and K-Q (winning about 43%) than against A-K and Q-10 (winning about 37%), because of the lack of duplication. One trick to avoid getting into trouble with J-J is to pretend it's 8-8. You'll only play it hard in favourable post-flop situations, and won't try to beat the world with it, pre-flop.

● Q-Q: The third best starting hand in hold'em should be played aggressively. The problem in low-limit games is you won't just be up against one player holding A-K: You'll be up against K-10 here and A-9 there, and that's much less favourable than facing a solitary A-K. In no limit, what sort of hands will you face heavy action with? Bluffs, the occasional person overplaying a smaller pair or A-Q, A-K... and K-K or A-A, where you're a 9/2 underdog. It's often best to make a significant but not full-commitment raise and wait to see if the flop contains an Ace or King. If you're in a tournament, and someone raises up front, someone else moves in on him, and someone else calls

the all-in bet, unless at least one of the all-in players was short stacked, your Queens belong in the muck. Ditto where someone seems unafraid of multiple opponents.

● K-K: 'Cowboys' are a terrific hand and worth playing quite strongly. They do belong a full level below Aces, though, because even some rookie playing A-3 has a 30% chance to beat you with his overcard. In a low-limit, multi-way pot, if an Ace flops, your Kings are essentially doomed; only in high-limit games where players will throw hands like A-9 away do you have a chance, and even then, it's probably worth not bothering until you're an advanced player. Try to avoid going on tilt when the Kings get beaten, because players hold singleton Aces a lot and 30% chances aren't insignificant.

Aces in the hole

● A-A: 'Pocket rockets' are much better than Kings because you can't be facing an overcard. One key in playing Aces correctly lies in knowing when to get away from them. In low-limit, multi-way games, you should figure that two red aces are toast when the flop comes 9♠, 10♠, J♠; in other words,

> **One way to avoid getting into trouble with pocket Jacks is to pretend they're pocket eights. Don't try to beat the world with them, pre-flop**

PERILOUS PLAYS

Hold or fold? You won't know what your pocket pair is *really* worth until the flop

Pocket pairs are usually the best hand before the flop, but remember that in hold'em, one's hand is usually defined by the flop, when you see three cards all at once. One of the biggest mistakes players make with pocket pairs is getting stubborn with them once the flop makes it probable they are no longer leading. Remember, hold'em is a seven-card game, not a two-card game.

Because low pocket pairs almost always have to flop a set to be worth continued play, it's vitally important to keep position in mind when playing. If you are the first player to act and hold a small pair, there is a strong chance that you will face one or more raises by the time the action gets back to you, and then the price to see the flop isn't right. You'll only flop a set one time in eight tries, so try to get in there cheaply, and try to get in against opponents who have enough money to pay you off handsomely if you get lucky.

beware extremely coordinated flops. Don't get stubborn. A lot of no-limit players like to limp with Aces, hoping that someone else will raise, and then they can re-raise. But if five people wind up limping, you have no idea where you are after the flop. You raise a lot with other hands and get re-raised; why not raise with this one, and hope you get re-raised here? If everyone folds and you just win the blinds, that's unfortunate, but not as bad as losing your whole stack because you let someone in too cheaply and only bet heavily once his hand became well defined. ✿

In the bluff

Clever bluffers can leave you feeling naked – like they've seen right through you.
Poker expert **Phil Shaw** explains how to avoid being caught with your trousers down

The most famous aspect of poker, but also the most misunderstood, is bluffing. From the glamour of Hollywood films to the many myths surrounding famous players, bluffing is always the key element invoked to sum up what poker is supposed to be about – a romantic fantasy of getting something for nothing, living off your wits by infallibly reading all an opponent's tells, and, of course, winning again and again in situations where you would have exactly the same chances of doing so as your opponent if the cards were all face up.

Of course, this isn't quite the case. As in physics, where 'every action has an equal and opposite reaction', in poker there's a whole flip side to bluffing that poker players must understand, whether they're calling a bluff and winning with next to nothing,

laying 'the great American bear trap' and inducing an opponent into making that one fatal move, or just practising damage limitation.

As we'll see, these are the essential dynamics of poker. They're also what makes it as exciting to watch or play as any other game in which the impetus swings backwards and forwards rapidly while the players do their best to impose order on the chaos, consistently pushing things in their favour, all the while knowing they can overbalance at any time and do exactly the opposite.

Horses for courses...

Poker is a game of people as well as probabilities, and each player is a different riddle waiting to be solved in order to come up with the right plan of attack. Since bluffing is one of your

main weapons, it's crucial to know not only the different types of bluff on offer to you (see the Know Your Bluffs box, page 38) but how, when and if to use them against different players.

Thanks to Alan Sccoonmaker's seminal book *The Psychology of Poker*, most players can be characterised in general terms along sliding scales of loose to tight and passive to aggressive, which gives four generally recognised types of player, plus other 'special' categories. When you sit in a poker game, either online or live, you need to watch your opponents' betting patterns and behaviour to decide ➤

Even the loose-aggressive maniacs get some good cards, and if you read a situation wrongly, they will often cost you all you have

KNOW YOUR BLUFFS!

Bluffing is the act of making a bet with the worst hand, and hopefully forcing an opponent to fold a better one. Easy enough in principle, but when it comes to Texas hold'em, you also need to know the various ways you can do this successfully. So here are some of the many types of bluff on offer to you, as well as a few of the basic counter tactics!

Semi-bluff

This is when you're 'betting with outs' – that is, if you do get called, you still have ways to win, such as betting a flush draw in the knowledge that you may win with a bluff or still make the flush if you get called. This tactic is used frequently by the pros and all good players, and is often the deadliest, as it means your opponents will find it difficult to know if you have a strong hand or just a draw any time you put chips in pot.

Naked bluff

A naked bluff is when you're 'betting without outs' knowing that the only way you can win is if you make the other player fold. Daring and audacious, this is a very high-risk option that requires a precise 'read' on

your opponents and a lot of guts. John Duthie put on a master class of naked bluffs to win £1 million at the inaugural Poker Million in 2001, although one reason he got away with it is that he never had to show any of them, and the other players didn't have a clue until afterwards!

Rebluff

Sensing that someone else is making a move in a pot and fighting back to try to beat them at their own game is known as a rebluff. Often called 'the strongest move in poker', this is an ultra-high-risk, sophisticated play made by many top players mainly against other top players, all of whom understand intimately the 'levels inside levels' that are present in a high-stakes poker game.

Delayed bluff

A less spectacular version of the rebluff, the delayed bluff consists of calling a bet with nothing against a seemingly weak opponent, with the intention of taking the pot away on a later betting round. This often works best with position, as if you call a bet on the flop or turn last and then the other player fails to follow through, it frequently means they were stealing. Moreover, if you either called and missed a draw or called with nothing just to bluff later, you've found a great low-risk opportunity to do so.

Positional bluff

A positional bluff is using good table position to exert pressure on the opposition. You may be raising to steal the blinds in late position, or betting one of the subsequent rounds in the hope that you can make a player pass a better hand when they know you will be acting after them throughout, and could put them to some tough decisions.

Check-raise bluff

Checking to let your opponent bet after you with position, and then re-raising is a check-raise bluff. This is both a high risk and a very powerful move, as the check-raise almost always signifies strength, meaning you might force an opponent to fold. Equally, though, if they call or re-raise, then you've created a big pot out of position and are left with the equally tough choices of giving up or making an even bigger and potentially fatal bluff on the next betting round.

Trap

A trap is feigning weakness with a very strong hand in the hope that an opponent will make an ill-timed bluff. This might be through 'slow play', where you check and call other players' bets, or a small bet that hopes to communicate weakness and bring a raise or bluff from an opponent.

Check-call

An antidote to very aggressive players and a way of minimising your damage if you fear you've walked into a hand rather than a bluff, check-calling means simply calling down an opponent when you think they have nothing. If you're right, then the other player has effectively given a lot of free chips to you, and if you are wrong, at least you found out as cheaply as possible.

➤ what general types they are so you can play against them effectively. You also have to be prepared to constantly review your opinions and watch out for those clever souls who want to mislead you into hanging their name on the wrong peg.

LOOSE-PASSIVE

The proverbial 'calling station' or 'mug that you can't bluff', this type of player hardly ever raises or takes the lead in a hand, but plays so badly as to not even understand the basic concepts and just blindly calls with any kind of a hand. Often, embarrassingly unobservant players try to force them to fold only to find themselves losing to a pair of deuces!

Also best labelled as 'tricky' players, the tight-aggressive types usually also have a sophisticated understanding of the game

This type of player will almost never win, as they have the whole ethos of poker back to front. As such, all you have to do to beat them is bet your good hands, throw away the bad ones and avoid looking like an idiot by trying to 'get fancy' against them.

TIGHT-PASSIVE

The 'rock' in the game who has the entire table folding as soon as he reaches for his chips is tight-passive. They play so few hands and raise so infrequently that the idea of them having anything less than a huge hand is inconceivable. This type of player is your ideal candidate for bluffing, as they usually pass a hand if you so much as reach for chips. Of course, you must bluff subtly and with some randomness or risk being discovered and antagonise them into a different pattern of play. However, if you manage this balancing act, all you have to do is fold at the least sign of strength from them and steal as much as possible the rest of the time.

LOOSE-AGGRESSIVE

The 'maniac' who sits in your game raising and re-raising every pot is the embodiment of this category. This type of player seems intent on creating as much action as possible and views a bet or raise like a bull views a red rag, irrespective of whether it ultimately leads to their own downfall of not.

Loose-aggressive players can produce carnage in a tournament if enough opponents employ the wrong tactics and give them a lot of chips or if they get out in front through luck, so you must bide you time and wait for good hands in the hope of getting paid off. You can lower your standards a little when playing hands against them and try a few more speculative holdings in the knowledge that you're likely to win chips. Don't go too far, though, as even the maniacs get good cards, and if you read a situation wrongly, they can cost you dear.

TIGHT-AGGRESSIVE

The 'stone killer' is the category into which most of the best players fall most of the time. They don't play many hands and so earn respect from the other players for this, but also look to maximise their win rate when they do get involved by betting draws, check-raising, trapping and using any other strategies they see fit. Also best labelled as 'tricky' players, the tight-aggressive types usually also have a sophisticated understanding of the game. These players mix all of the various elements of success, and can vary them to create a smoke screen or false 'image'.

For example, a tight-aggressive player might often play loose-aggressive when they think the time is right, or feign an element of passivity in the knowledge that they can use this later against players who are too eager to jump to conclusions and categorise them as easy touches. Needless to say, this is the style you should be most looking to emulate, and the type of player you least want to be up against in marginal situations.

'SPECIAL' CATEGORIES

These players seem to defy traditional definition, and when they're good, they often fall clearly outside of the tight-aggressive box. For example, one recognisable type these days is the good loose-aggressive player. These guys play many hands with devastating force, but always have an acute idea of where they are at in any

given situation, and can just as easily make staggering bluffs or fold if they end up in a situation they don't like. Meanwhile, of course, they're also plotting to take all your chips when they do pick up a monster.

Recently, 'Gambling' Gus Hansen has been the embodiment of this style – he will raise with any two cards as he's so busy playing the opponent that what he has himself hardly matters – but there's a long tradition of truly great players of this type, including Doyle Brunson, Stu Ungar and Ted Forrest.

A game of situations and players

Now that we've looked at the basics of bluffing, including broad player categories, types of bluff and some counter strategies, it's time to get a bit

Very short-stacked players may call out of desperation, so if you have a lot of chips, you can still bully your way to winning a lot of pots

more complex and think about the specific circumstances that might allow you to make a successful bluff or catch an unconvincing one. We'll also look at some player types in more detail and figure out what makes them tick (see box, page 41). There are many questions to ask in doing this, and success often involves making a split-second appraisal of all the information and deciding on a course of action, which is why poker is so much fun. The following are the most important questions in poker:

What does your opponent have and what do they think you have?

If you could always answer these questions, you'd be unbeatable. However, aspiration is the best you can do, so remember from the outset that successful poker (and successful bluffing) revolves around reading your opponent's hand and always disguising your own.

What type of game is it and how many players are there?

The fewer players there are in a game or hand, the more bluffing becomes an option. Similarly, if you can make big ➤

➤bets as in no-limit hold'em, bluffing is much more likely to succeed than in limit hold'em. If you want to get a real feel for this aspect of the game, log on to one of the many online sites that offer heads-up (that is, one-on-one) no-limit hold'em tournaments and play a few. You'll soon find that waiting for a great hand and anteing away your chips is no fun, whereas raising, bluffing or calling with almost any two cards is a great way of sharpening your instincts as well as providing a real thrill.

What positions do your opponents occupy?

This has been covered before, but bears repeating. If you're in position, of course, bluffing is a potent weapon, as you hold all the power in the hand. If you're not in position, though, your play should be more defensive unless you're sure of exactly what's going on or you have a great hand.

What's your table image?

While you've been assessing the other players, it's likely they've all being doing exactly the same to you. So if you have a tight-cautious image, you're much more likely to be able to bluff

successfully (and be the target of bluffs), whereas if you've been playing fast and loose, or have been caught bluffing recently, the opposite is true.

Is the bluff convincing?

Against weak, bluffable opponents, the chances are you won't have to bet much or with great thought to win a hand with nothing. However, against good players, who understand the game and are often fearless, you need to make a bluff convincing and think it out incisively, representing a specific hand and playing exactly as you would

if you actually held it. This could mean sticking your neck out with a large all-in or facing a hand you suspect might be a bluff for big money, so there really is little margin for error!

At this point, there's usually a lot to consider (as this entire article makes clear). What it often boils down to, though, is whether you believe the player who is putting you to the test and, if not, whether you have the heart to follow your instincts and make a great call, or whether from the other side of the issue you believe you can put a move on an opponent.

Am I getting in too deep?

Remember that what you think could be a great move may actually be about to land you in someone else's trap. Always consider how much damage you stand to sustain if you get it wrong and play into someone else's hands or bottle it along the way and make your actions transparent. For this reason, check-raising with marginal hands, making big bluffs on the end and so on are not usually recommended for beginners. Similarly, you should be trying to condition the other players to get out of line in these ways when you do have a hand.

How big is the bet?

Whether bluffing or facing a potential bluff, this is one of the key pieces of information to consider. If you bet too little in relation to the size of the pot, you're normally more likely to get called, while if you over-bet, the odds you give the opposition are so slight they're likely to fold all but the best hands. However, skilful players know this and often reverse or randomise the bet size to add an element of confusion to the proceedings, and many great players are capable of putting in enormous bets and being equally likely to have the nuts or nothing.

What are the stack sizes?

Stack sizes are particularly important in a tournament when considering a bluff. Tournament chips change value

➤ throughout the event – if you win all the chips, you'll likely only get about 30-50% of the money, but if you lose your £100 buy-in, then the chips cost that plus the entry fee. As such, big stacks can bluff and call bluffs easily but short stacks can't, and you should play accordingly.

Remember, though, that some very short-stacked players may call out of desperation, and that if you have a lot of chips in reserve and aren't afraid to use them, you can still bully your way to winning a lot of pots even against moderate or big stacks.

What's the texture of the board?

It's sometimes difficult to bluff successfully when there are lots of draws on the flop or when you raise pre-flop and the flop comes all small cards. In the first instance, you might get called by a draw or a made hand; in the second, your opponent might stay with you unless they're convinced you have a big pair.

By contrast, scare cards can be a great chance to bluff – if your opponent seems to really hate the Ace that came on the flop, the chances are

Against good players, who understand the game and are often fearless, you need to make a bluff convincing and think it out incisively

you can successfully represent it, and the same is true if the turn or river card looks to have completed a flush or straight draw.

Is it a bluff or a value bet?

This is particularly important on the river, when there are no more cards to come. It's absolutely essential to your success that you learn to get a high percentage of these calls correct, and make the right decision if you have the option to bet. Again, there's no easy way of doing this other than by experience, but this is a great aspect of your game on which to work, as you'll always be considering the play of a complete hand and have all the info that goes with it, as well as being able to rule out the possibility of semi-bluffs.

At all times, remember that vital point: poker is a game of situations and players and well as one of cards and mathematics. Study all of these factors and you'll be well on your way to becoming a successful player. ✿

KNOW YOUR ENEMIES

If you're going to bluff, value bet and trap with the best of them, you'd better have a pretty good idea of who you're up against. Now that we've discussed the basic types of player (loose-aggressive, tight-aggressive, tight-passive and loose-passive) and given you some basic tactics with which to play against them, you should be well equipped. Here, we'll look at some of the more specific types of player to be found out there, and how you can deal with them to ensure success

Rank amateur

This player knows so little that they're barely speaking the same language as you in poker terms. In the words of David 'the Devilfish' Ulliott: 'if they don't know what they're doing how can you?' Proceed with care and beware of playing big pots when you don't have a big hand. Over time, you're sure to figure out a way to beat them, but meanwhile you might get a nasty surprise on any given hand!

Bully

An extension of the loose-aggressive player, this player looks for those who are weak, and often cares little about whether the outcome for themselves is triumph or disaster. The bully can be a top player if they channel the aggression and employ good judgement (as having control of the whole table is a great way of accumulating chips), or a mediocre one if they try to settle personal scores from previous hands, or demonstrate they're likely to 'blow off' a big stack. Decide which type they are and act accordingly.

A-Z game player

Many reputedly 'great' players who have earned their reputations through dazzling displays of talent are also prone to being temperamental for

whatever reason. For example, try to guess who 'not only has a B game, but also a C, D, E, F, G and so on game', and who 'when he's playing badly really stinks, making awful, borderline, amateurish decisions'. We wouldn't want to embarrass them here, but the moral of the story is to know when a player is performing below par and look for the right way to take advantage of it.

On tilt player

Rather than just playing below par, this player is visibly off the rails, whether it's down to alcohol, a bad beat or fear of the high stakes. The point is that they're temporarily incapable of making good decisions, so when you have a hand, give them as many as possible to contend with and hope it pays off.

ABC player

Those who clearly play 'by the book' are more prevalent in limit games, where imagination is less valuable than solid maths. In these situations, this type of player is likely to be highly predictable in starting hands and the way they repeat certain patterns. Respect the seemingly obvious plays they make, and look for ways to exploit them by thinking and playing outside the box.

Instinct/maths player

Often split between the no-limit and limit camps, this player type clearly values one approach over another. The instinct player believes they can make almost psychic assessments of their opponents cards and future actions, while the maths player believes everything can be solved though complex analysis. If you know a player clearly relies on one of these approaches, then do your best to exploit their blind side.

Young gun

It's often been said that as poker players grow old, they slow down a bit in terms of wildness and aggression, so bear the age of your opponent in mind when deciding whether to bluff or trap. For example, the young Scandinavian players are now famous for a hyper-aggressive relentless style, and knowing this could save you a few early bets.

Gambler

The 'action player' is different from the bully or the loose-aggressive player in that they're really just there for the thrill of the action. This player will likely give you the money in the end if you're patient.

Recreational player

This type of player considers the money they lose as payment for entertainment or lessons, and should be treated with respect and made to feel part of the game so they continue to take part. That's often the hard part for socially inept poker professionals, whereas figuring out ways to win against them is relatively easy, as they often don't put up much of a fight.

Chameleon

This is the ultimate opponent, with no definable characteristics nor patterns other than constant change and adaptation to circumstances, and a deep and rounded knowledge of the game. Ask a top player a poker question and they'll more often than not say: 'It depends'. While this can be frustrating, it's all too true. The reason for this is that poker is a game of situations and players. If you know an opponent might be playing any number of styles at a given point, how can you come up with a strategy to defeat them? The chameleon is the type of player you should be aspiring to be, but avoid them in a hand unless you have good reason not to.

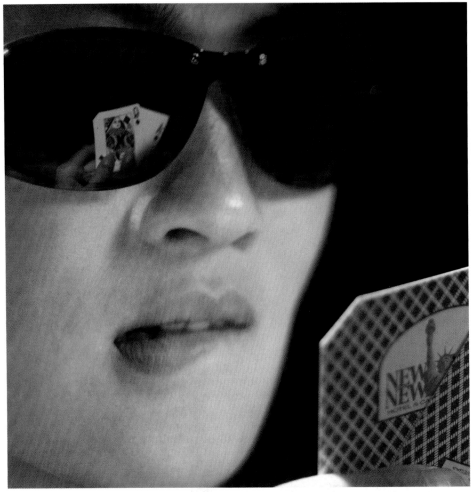

GIVING THE GAME AWAY

Expressions, tics, sighing... these are all signs your opponents make and which you can read to help your game. **Phil Shaw** lets you in on the top ten tells

Whether you play poker online, in home games or in a club or casino, there is much more to the game than just card values and ranking hands. As you'll have learned from previous poker articles, understanding factors such as position, how your opponents play, choosing the right games and self-discipline are all huge money-winners.

But the key factor is a 'tell': an unconscious indication from an opponent that reveals to you the strength of their hand or how they are likely to act. And if you know the gesture another player makes before folding, it doesn't matter what cards you have – you can win a pot easily. And if you know that they hold the 'nuts', you can save a fortune! Tells come in numerous forms, so

you must learn to read each player as well as remembering the general rules.

These rules have been set in stone since Mike Caro published his book *Caro's Book of Poker Tells*, in which he covers most areas of interest as well as distinguishing between 'tells from those who are unaware' and 'tells from actors'.

Caro explains that, with players putting on an act, 'weak means strong and vice versa'– if a player acts weak, they have a strong hand and if they try to display strength, the opposite is generally true.

This book is essential reading for any poker player and is still the main body of writing on the

Tells come in numerous forms, so you must learn to read each player

subject. Read and re-read it – most of today's serious players have certainly done so.

In addition to figuring out who the actors and the unaware are, modern poker players have to figure out who has read the book and will try to confuse observers with 'fake' or 'reverse' tells. So it's very important to take players on a case-by-case basis and try to understand from their actions how sophisticated they are. For example, a newcomer to the local $5 beginners' game who bets any two cards and calls with any pair or gutshot is unlikely to be giving out reverse tells. But a pro, who sits looking nervous and seems to

swallow a lot when in a hand with you, may well be selling a line. Once you have some idea of what level the other players are at, you can figure out what their possible tells mean.

When most pros talk about making a difficult read, they usually mention sensing extreme weakness or strength as the key factor. As they are so good at taking in all the available information and deciding what it means they don't consciously need to look for it.

For the beginner or average player, though, this sixth sense takes time to develop. There's no substitute for experience. To give you a head start, however, here are the top ten areas to look at. Just remember to beware of anyone tricky enough to try and send you the wrong way!

1 EYES

They are so easy to read that many players wear sunglasses in a game, while others complain that wearing them is cheating. As everyone knows, the windows of the soul can tell you how someone is feeling, if a partner is being truthful, or if they really did win on the horses that afternoon. Recently at the Heads Up stage of the Paris World Poker Tour, Tony G was so dismayed with Surrinder Sunar for ignoring him that he got down on the floor next to him and tried to peer behind his opponent's glasses in search of a reaction.

Watching the eyes can be a major earner. Caro says glancing at someone or staring for an unusually long time can be a sign of a bluff. He adds that a player who looks away is a much greater threat than one who watches what is happening (as they don't want to discourage a bet), and that a quick glance at their chips after checking their cards or the board is a key sign that a player has something powerful.

2 CHIPS

Does a player stack their chips neatly or leave them splashed over the felt in front of them? Do they build precarious skyscrapers with them or solid, fortress-like enclosures? These are the kinds of things that might give away the way a player is feeling or their general mentality. Of course, this is one of the easiest tells to reverse, so it shouldn't be taken too seriously. But other aspects of chip handling are sometimes important.

For example, a player who puts chips in a pot in several different ways might be subconsciously telling you something each time, whereas the way someone acts with them in response to you might also be key. One commonly known tell is the 'threat beat', where as soon as you look likely to bet your opponent picks up a huge pile of chips hoping to scare you off. Players who riffle their chips or do tricks with them are also giving away valuable information, even if it's only something as simple as indicating that they have previous poker experience or want to gain some authority over the table.

3 FACIAL TELLS

Nervous twitches, frowns, smiles, furrowings of the brow and itches that just have to be scratched are some of the most revealing areas, yet also the easiest and most popular to fake or reverse. For example, next time you find yourself faced with a tough decision, consider whether the opponent really looks like they had to scratch their head as a comforting device, or if the action is contrived and ostentatious. Similarly, if you watch a televised event, you might consider whether the Pokerbrat was covering his mouth out of a subconscious need to conceal a lie (bluffing), whether it was an act designed to suggest the opposite, or whether it was even a 'double bluff' trying to back up the steal attempt!

4 PROPS/COMFORTING DEVICES

Many players smoke or drink during a hand, but what does the way or time they do this signify? Is the way they exhale smoke a release of tension or do they savour the next drag as they prepare to move in for the kill? Do they gulp down water in an attempt to repress a bad beat or in a way that indicates that they might be about to leave the table?

If they're drinking, how much have they had and is this next one likely to take them over the edge? In the film *Rounders,* John Malkovich's character Teddy KGB was revealed as having a disastrous Oreos-related tell. While your local game sure isn't Hollywood, the props and comforting devices that people transfer emotions to are key to understanding their play.

Similarly, many players eat at the table, and a player who looks at his cards and goes back to his meal isn't likely to be interested in anything but his belly. Other players have chip markers or lucky charms which they toy with, or riffle their chips as a way of releasing tension. If you can figure out why they interact with their props at any given moment, it could make you a fortune.

5 POSTURE

Does a player sink into their seat or sit up very straight in response to a bet or looking at the cards? Do they appear relaxed or nervous, are they agitated or still? These factors are observed by everyone, but they may tell you whether a player is disconnected or involved from a poker game, if they are in the zone or nervous and unlikely to bet without a strong hand. Similarly, you can observe whether players check one card at a time or both, or if they need to look back at their cards occasionally (maybe when a flush becomes possible on a hold'em board) and how they subsequently react.

7 VOICE

The road gamblers of old would often say that they could read a man's hand from the way that he spoke. And today, even for the inexperienced, what a player says and how they sound can be a great way of determining what they are holding. In a televised event, you will often see a player ask someone how much he has left when you can be sure he has a fair idea and just wants to hear the opponent speak.

Similarly, the way in which a player says: 'Raise' or 'All-in' can be indicative of where they're at in the hand. In a game such as no-limit hold'em, where players often play a draw like a made hand, this can be vital information. And listen to any other comments they make, try to figure out what they want you to do – then do the opposite!

6 HANDS

Along with the eyes, the most revealing parts of the body are the hands. They may express impatience through tapping on the table, the forward gesture of a powerful all-in, or be used to put chips in a variety of motions. The best-known piece of information about them is that when a player's hands begin to shake violently this often means they have a superb holding – although this must be qualified in the context of the situation. An internet qualifier playing in their first major event might have hands that shake every time they pick up their cards!

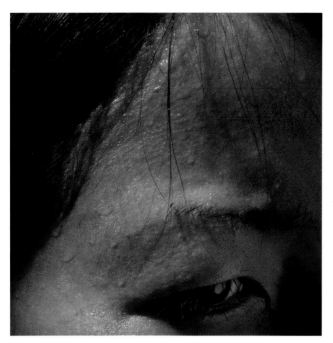

8 HEARTBEAT

Everyone has seen the fun that can be had from novel innovations, such as the TV show *Poker Million's* use of heart-rate monitors, whereby viewers can tell which internet qualifier is thinking about their mortgage, which circuit regular needs a new health regime and why certain sporting personalities are relentless achievers.

Observing heartbeat and blood pressure-related tells can be key information for the pros. A player whose breathing has started to resemble that of an Olympic athlete is clearly not in a normal internal state; similarly, it is difficult to fake calmness when your neck vein is beating like a heavy-metal drummer and your brow is sweating like you've got a fever. Both of these tells can be reliable signs of a bluff and even concern some of the best players since they are often involuntary. It's not unheard of for high-profile players worried about the latter of these giveaways to spend a whole tournament wearing a neck scarf.

9 BETTING PATTERNS

Most poker players rely on logic as much as their reads of other players, and people tend to repeat the same motions. So if a player regularly overbets the nuts or checks the turn when bluffing, this might be as worthwhile an observation as all the others put together. A tell is just a piece of information that reveals the strength of your opponent's hand. If you find an area in which they repeatedly show weakness or strength by betting certain amounts, or betting in certain ways, then you've struck gold.

10 INTERNET/LIVE TELLS

Tells exist much less on the internet than in live games, but even online a new set of tells are created by the environment itself. Pre-action buttons for checking (where players tick a box and the action is taken in turn) can be a great sign against unsophisticated opponents that all you have to do to win is bet. And, with the absence of visual information, the speed of betting becomes a more salient factor. This is true in a live game as well, but online people are so much more likely to be multi-tasking – making coffee or playing in several games at once – that it is often more reliable there.

Similarly, if a player pauses for an abnormal period before raising or calling, you have seen something interesting. Do they have a tough decision to make or are they trying to reel you in (particularly likely if they then raise)? Alternatively, do they think you are attentive enough to be watching out for and recording their moves?

Screen names or avatars are also an interesting factor online, since the global nature of internet poker might throw you together with opponents for only short periods of time and you will have to make quick assessments. For example, people with gangster personas may either be there for business purposes or to pose; the supermodel picture may actually disguise a 25-stone truck driver from Skegness, and while 'PhillyHelmuth' probably isn't who the name suggests it is, 'Neverwin' really isn't a guy you want to play shorthanded $100/$200 hold'em with! ❈

The art of living dangerously

Sometimes, poker hands which look good at first glance can blow up in your face. But never fear – **Phil 'Dangerous' Shaw** is here to make sure you don't get your fingers burned...

Danger hands in poker are the ones that you either shouldn't be playing in the first place – but do because they look seductive, fun or profitable (shortly before getting you into trouble) – or they're ones which have massive potential, usually either to win you a lot of money or lose you a lot.

Below is a list of some of the most misplayed hands in hold'em, and some of the ways in which people commonly go wrong. Bear in mind that poker is a game of situations, people and position: a hand that's easy to play (or fold) in one situation could present a different problem in another.

Winning at poker is therefore all about making good (or great) decisions. To do this, a poker player needs to be an expert in laying and taking odds, or knowing when to refuse a bet, in complex situations. They can do this with some margin for error and accept some risks, but overall each decision gives them a small edge which over time adds up to serious financial gain.

If you're playing a no-limit Texas hold'em tournament and you're dealt 8♣-3♥ in first position, you don't have much of a decision – you pass it quickly. But that's not profitable. Profitable decisions come in situations where you play a hand better that almost everyone else, whether you pass, call or raise with it. In our hypothetical tournament, it would be equally obvious what to do with A-A or A-K if you only had a small number of chips left – you would stick them all-in and hope to win the hand and survive.

But what about finding a danger hand in that situation if instead you have lots of chips left – for example A-9 OS, 7-8 S, Q-J OS or even J-J? Now, your decision is a lot tougher.

Each of these hands has a generally optimum way of being played in first position (fold, call, fold, raise) which will make you some profit in the long term, and you will need to have a good idea of what this is. But it also depends on exactly where you are in a specific game – is it the re-buy period, is someone on tilt, are many players likely to call? Whether you see the opportunity to be a little creative by doing something slightly different comes into play, too, as does finding what Howard Lederer calls: 'A profitable way to stray from what would generally be considered the proper play.'

> **If you always play a hand in the same way, people will recognise it, and your game will become transparent**

The reason for doing this is that if you always play a hand in the same way, people will recognise it, and your game will become transparent. Therefore, raising with the suited connectors or check-raising with the Jacks might be more profitable occasionally. But just bear in mind that by doing this, you increase the risk of serious harm if your plan backfires, and that danger hands before the flop can become nightmares after it when played like this. If such a situation develops when you slow-play a monster or push a marginal hand too far, you should simply remember that the first mistake is often the easiest to walk away from, and that such cards are called danger hands for a reason.

A-A

The 'American Airlines' can look as appealing as a flight to the Bahamas, but beginners are often found at the bar, complaining that they not only cost them their luggage but their shirt as well. Because a hold'em hand consists of five cards from seven overall but only two pre-flop, the value of Aces is massive early on. However, it drops soon afterwards as the flop might give someone two pair or trips, and may present a straight or flush draw for the turn or river to complete.

In contrast, the bets in no-limit or pot-limit games are smallest at the start and escalate rapidly from there. So other players are often getting the 'implied odds' they need to call pre-flop and try to make a better hand or draw before setting about taking your money.

For this reason, Aces need to be played strong early to deny others the implied odds and to leave you with a good idea of what any callers might have made on the flop. So if you raise with a good portion of your chips and the flop comes K♥, 5♦, 2♥, after which you and your one opponent go to war, you can be fairly confident of being ahead.

If you just called – looking for a check-raising opportunity that didn't come – and several players get involved, you could be facing any number of hands that are now ahead or could be by the river.

J-J

The 'Hooks' are called that for more than one reason, as they can reel you into losing a fortune and are generally regarded as one of the most difficult hands to play in hold'em. If you raise with them and are called, the chances are that the flop will contain one or more overcards. And even if it doesn't, there is always the danger of then losing a fortune to Aces, Kings or Queens. If someone re-raises you, it's likely that they hold either a bigger pair or overcards, such as A-K or A-Q, so you are either a small favourite or a big dog.

In poker, this is a situation you are constantly trying to avoid, so Jacks more than any pair are like chameleons. For example, if you know someone often plays small pairs or weak Aces, they can be a great hand to come over the top with. However, if there has already been a raise and a re-raise to you, in most games you would sooner light a fire with them than get involved.

2-2

Small pairs are often overplayed in limit games, or by people who ignore the cardinal rule of no-limit tournament all-ins, which is to get the money in when either 50/50 or better. If you think about it, when you are holding 2-2 to do this, an opponent's hand would also have to contain a deuce, and they could also have a better pair, making you around a 9/2 dog!

All small pairs are best avoided late in tournaments unless you are in late position and face many callers or only a very small raise. They are playable early in big-bet tournaments or cash games where the money is deep. But once you get to the flop, you should follow the advice of Tom McEvoy and TJ Cloutier: 'No set, no bet.'

A-X OFF-SUIT

The weak Ace is exactly what it sounds like in most situations, despite some players and commentators' predilections to get excited about it. If you raise and are re-raised, you are forced to fold, and if you get to the flop to see an Ace you may have 'kicker trouble'. Similarly, hitting the low kicker is rarely enough to continue in the hand, and you will frequently miss altogether.

In short, then, it's one of the main danger hands in hold'em and unless you're an expert, you play it at your peril. Remember, a hand with a hole in it is frequently worse than no hand at all (with no hand you lose no money). Playing the weak Ace after the flop can often feel like the equivalent of walking around with one leg broken.

Depending on the level of game you play in – and your opponents' care of choice over kickers – it will need to be calibrated differently though. For example, against loose, weak opponents who play any Ace, A-10 or A-J could easily be enough to ensure success, whereas a player such as Doyle Brunson describes even A-Q as being a trouble hand in many situations.

Q-J OFF-SUIT

Although face cards may look pretty and appealing, they can often get you into trouble and leave you feeling sick afterwards. That's why John Duthie described getting excited about them as 'suffering from a disease'. The reason is that although they are high cards they are always losing to any Ace pre-flop, and can frequently be in a tight spot if the Ace's kicker 'duplicates' one of them (such as K-Q vs A-Q), especially if played all-in.

They are moderate, defensive hands if you need to act in a hurry, and they are playable in late position or if suited. However, just don't fall for the impression that a nice paint job means you're guaranteed to find sound engineering underneath.

9-8 SUITED

Suited connectors, such as 9♠-8♠ or 6♦-7♦, can be useful hands as long as they're played carefully and cheaply. That's because no one will ever suspect a straight on a flop of 6, 7, 10, or a monster draw on one of A♦, 5♠, 6♦. However, they also suffer from the slim possibility of putting you in a complete lock against a higher straight or flush and guaranteeing you lose all your chips.

This danger is most apparent either very early during big tournaments, or in deep cash games, otherwise the odds will be usually be in your favour – but when it happens it's nothing less than a complete disaster!

Making the lower flush is a danger you will struggle to avoid when you're playing this type of hand. But, with straight draws, you need to remember what other hands you could be running into. For example, 8-9 S looks great with a flop of 10, J, Q, until someone turns up A-K.

Similarly, as soon as higher cards start competing your draw, they are also likely either to be making a better one for someone else or hitting them directly and making you a favourite to be bet out of the hand.

Know the odds

While tournament poker is a game of situations and psychology, do your maths homework and you'll be leaving less to chance. Human calculator **Phil Shaw** examines the odds and reveals the most common confrontations with percentages to help maximise your chances when it counts

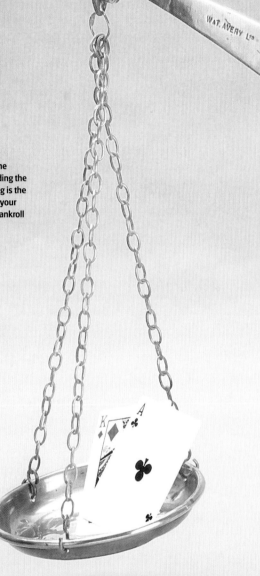

▶ Weighing up the odds: understanding the number-crunching is the key to improving your game and your bankroll

Every time you make a decision or respond to what another player does in poker you are taking and laying odds. While a game like no-limit hold'em often comes down to a 'Do they have it or don't they' scenario, there are many games and situations in poker where the odds alone that you are getting on a hand will dictate your action. For example, in a game like limit hold'em or Omaha many of the decisions you make will be highly mathematical ones based on the 'pot odds', and in some situations there might even be no point trying to bluff a player because of the odds, whereas in others you could virtually call blind.

It's therefore important to have a strong idea of the odds of making or defending your hand in any given situation, and the ability to quickly compare them to the 'pot odds' you are getting or giving. Tournament poker, in particular, is one area where all top players know inside out the odds of their hand winning an all-in against other hands, because these confrontations come up so frequently. Most of them don't like playing all-ins that are close to even money, and some will even fold as a decent favourite rather than risk a big all-in early on, because they expect to have a better chance of outplaying amateurs in smaller pots. But even for the greats there comes a point in a

> In some situations there might even be no point trying to bluff a player because of the odds, in others you could call blind

tournament when playing an all-in is necessary, and – needless to say – you should always be looking to be a clear favourite when this happens.

Poker odds can be examined in a variety of ways, and we have split them into sections below to make the process easier, as well as listing some common confrontations with percentages for you to learn and remember. I've omitted odds from flop to turn, and on the turn, as these can simply be calculated by counting the outs for or against you out of the remaining cards.

BASIC ODDS

In hold'em there are 1,326 possible two-card combinations for your starting hand, and 1,225 for any one of your opponents after you look at your cards. If you play a hand through, there are then 19,600 possible flops and 2,118,760 total full-board combinations. This means that you could play for a lifetime and not see exactly the same thing happen twice!

With these parameters the chances of getting a pocket pair are 16/1, and of making it into trips or quads on the flop 12%. The chances of getting Aces are 220/1 against and A-K about 1.2%, and, given you don't have a pair, you will make one on the flop about one third of the time and about 49% of the time by the river. With suited cards,

TERMINOLOGY

Understand the basics or you'll never tell your good hands from your bad ones. Or your arse from your elbow

Basic Odds The odds of an occurrence based on just your cards or your hand played to completion. For example, the chances of getting dealt A-A pre-flop, or making your flush, of four of a kind coming on the board.

Pot Odds The amount a pot is laying you compared to the relative strength of your hand. So if a short-stacked tournament player moves all-in for 1,100 when the blinds are 500-1,000 and you are the solitary opponent on the big blind, you needn't even look at your cards before calling as you are getting 26/1 for your money, which is a magnificent price even if you turn over 2-7.

It's more complex if the sums are closer to even, for example if you're getting exactly 7/2 pot odds on the board pairing on the river when you have trips against what you're sure is a completed flush or straight (making you 3.4/1 against), and the other player is all-in. Here you would call in a cash game, as mathematically it's a profitable play, but in a tournament you may fold, as the small edge you have may not be worth risking a large chunk of money for – unless you want to gamble.

Implied Odds The money you expect to get from an opponent if you make your hand and betting continues. For example, a good player might think: 'I'm getting slightly less than the necessary pot odds to draw at the straight here, but I know that Tom is likely to pay me off afterwards if I make it, so it's worth my calling'.

> **If you never use reverse implied odds in relation to your game, it's a cause for self-congratulation**

To estimate this accurately you need a good sense of your opponent and his hand, as well as how the hand you make and your position are likely to affect the situation. For example, in hold'em if you called with a belly-buster straight draw, another player would be unlikely to realise if you made it, whereas in Omaha as soon as the board pairs or a three-flush comes it's highly likely someone has made the nuts or something close.

Reverse Pot Odds / Reverse Implied odds The amount it will cost you and you stand to lose afterwards by drawing at and making a second-best hand. Such as drawing to a straight when someone else already has a made flush, or either of these hands on a paired board where someone else already has a full house. If you never use these terms in relation to your game, it's a cause for major self-congratulation.

Redraws When estimating odds, consider the chances of making your draw but still being beaten when another hand also improves, such as by drawing to a straight, making it and losing to a newly-made flush or full house. Very important in Omaha, where the nuts can change on every street, and you often play on a street-by-street basis rather than trying to get all the money in early. For example, any decent Omaha player knows that a made straight on the flop is destined to lose when sandwiched between trips and a flush draw (or even a better straight draw) and should therefore be junked.

you will make a flush 8.4% of the time by the river but only flop a flush 0.84% of the time, and flop a flush draw nearly 11% of the time of which it will be completed with a frequency of 38.3%. If you flop an open-ended straight draw, it will complete 34% of the time. The flop will be all of one suit some 5% of the time, two suited cards 55% and rainbow 40%.

All of this is interesting to know, and there are many other interesting facts in poker, but often such information is of limited use since your equity in a situation also depends on what cards your opponents are holding in any given situation. Because of this, in some games (especially Omaha) you may ignore 'redraws' if only looking at one side of the equation and ➤

> overestimate your chances. On the other hand, you may be in a better position than you think. For example, in hold'em the chances of completing your flush draw after the flop are low, but if you also have a live Ace (see A♥-3♥ vs 9♠-9♦ in the Hand Match-Ups box below) they are much better.

So basic odds are certainly important, because they give you a framework to think within, but you mustn't forget that poker is also about situations and psychology as well as mathematics – so although the chances of any given player having Aces pre-flop in hold'em may be 220/1 against, unless they raise blind every hand, when they do raise the true odds are going to be a whole lot shorter.

PRE-FLOP, ALL-IN HAND MATCH-UPS

The key here is to spot hands that are likely to dominate, and those that are likely to be dominated. This is mainly useful for the purposes of tournament all-ins because a bad hand may be getting the odds to outdraw a good one on the flop and thereafter, but your equity in a pre-flop all-in is fixed and not affected by whatever the board throws up.

If you're considering a call, compare this information with the pot odds you're getting and decide if the risk is worth it with a marginal hand, and whether you're likely to be pot-committed if raising or facing a re-raise all-in.

Everyone is familiar with the concept of situations in hold'em where a pair takes on two overcards, and

Running a big pair into trips or going up against someone with two pair is likely to be disastrous for your bankroll

because these are unavoidable you should always be looking to get the money in during situations where you can be evens or better. For example, A-K may run up against A-Q as well as 8-8 and therefore be a good all-in investment, whereas the best 2-2 can hope for is overcards and a bigger pair would be a 9/2 against disaster. You can raise all-in but you cannot call an all-in with it.

Notice from the odds listed that the emphasis is therefore on drawing to 'live' cards in a showdown – such as with A-6 vs 7-7 only the A is a live out and in A-7 vs A-K only the 7 is live, putting both hands in very bad shape. When there are no pairs or duplications, things are much closer with A-K vs 8-9 S and A-J vs Q-9 being 3/2 shots, and middle connectors like 8-9 S vs A-4 being virtually evens shots.

ON THE FLOP

These odds demonstrate popular confrontations when all the money goes in on the flop and illustrates the importance of not risking a situation where you are a massive underdog. In order to do this you will need a good idea of what you are up against, which means protecting your hand pre-flop and understanding just how big a draw you have on the flop, as well as how your opponents play certain hands.

For example, if you have a combination hand like a live Ace and flush draw against a pair, a straight and flush draw, or a pair and a draw, you're

likely to be in reasonable shape unless of course you run into a monster, whereas the wrong end of a straight draw or a second-best flush could obviously cost you dear. Similarly, running a big pair into trips or going up against someone with two pair or a better pair is likely to be disastrous for your bankroll.

HAND MATCH-UPS

Check out this selection of hands and their odds of landing you the pot in heads-up play

PRE-FLOP

Hands	Win	Lose	Draw
A♣-A♦ vs K♠-K♣	81.5	18	0.5
A♣-A♦ vs Q♠-J♠	80	19.5	0.5
A♥-A♦ vs K♣-T♥	86	13.5	0.5
A♣-K♣ vs A♦-7♥	72.5	23	4.5
A♣-6♣ vs A♦-2♣	38	28	34
A♣-K♣ vs 2♥-2♣	50	49.5	0.5
A♣-K♣ vs Q♠-Q♣	43.5	56	0.5
A♥-K♣ vs 8♥-9♥	61	38.5	0.5
A♣-J♥ vs Q♣-9♣	58.5	41	0.5
A♣-6♣ vs 9♥-T♣	51.5	48	0.5

ON THE FLOP

Hands	Flop	Win	Lose	Draw
A♥-A♣ vs 9♣-9♦	7♠, 3♦, 2♥	91.5	8.5	
A♥-A♣ vs 9♣-9♦	9♠, 3♦, 2♥	10	90	
A♥-A♣ vs 7♣-8♣	9♣, 6♣, 2♣	56.5	43.5	
A♥-K♥ vs 9♣-9♦	7♥, 3♦, 2♥	45	55	
A♥-3♥ vs 9♠-9♦	7♥, 3♦, 2♥	47.5	52.5	
A♠-J♦ vs K♠-J♥	J♦, 4♣, 3♥	86.5	12	1.5
A♥-A♣ vs 9♠-7♣	6♥, 8♣, 2♣	66	34	
A♥-A♣ vs 9♣-7♣	9♣, 8♣, 6♣	33.5	64.5	2
A♥-A♣ vs 9♣-7♣	K♣, 2♣, 4♣	63.5	36.5	
9♣-9♥ vs A♣-3♣	A♥, 7♣, 4♦	9	91	

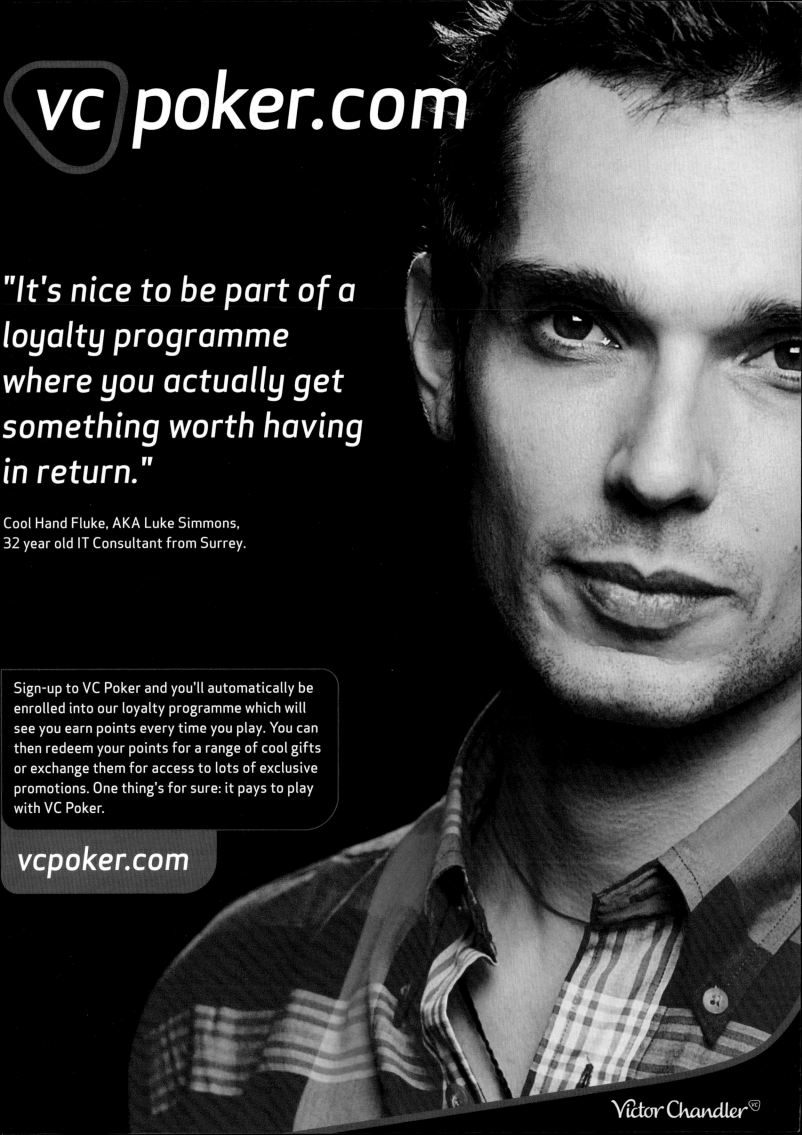

A nice position to be in

Where you're sitting in a game of poker can be crucial to making the most of your hand, with the button being the strongest seat of all. However, as **Phil Shaw** explains, there are ways to play any position to your advantage

Anyone who has ever watched *Late Night Poker* will be well aware of Jesse May's explanations of what the dealer button is. It is, of course, where the cards are dealt around from clockwise, starting on its immediate left, and it's where the dealer would be sitting in a self-dealt game. What, though, are the implications of this system and what does position – that is, where you're sitting relative to the dealer button – actually amount to in poker?

Well, first, you need to understand the mechanics of the game. In flop games, such as hold'em and Omaha, it's relatively simple: the button always moves in a clockwise direction and the players immediately to its left post the blinds, which are compulsory pre-flop bets that determine the amount to call or raise and mean there's always some money in the pot for which to play. Stud is different, and Omaha is sometimes played with one, two or three blinds so we're going to stick to hold'em for this article.

Blind man's bluff

Hold'em almost always has two blinds – the small blind and the big blind – with the small blind being immediately to the left of the dealer button and usually half the size of the big one. In a cash game, these will be fixed (for example, $1 or $2), and in a tournament they'll continue to rise so players are forced to act and the game reaches a conclusion. Whatever the format, the player to the left of the big blind (the under the gun player) acts first pre-flop, and then the small blind acts first in the three subsequent betting rounds. As such, the player on the button has the best position of all, as they're the last to act of those who have put no money in blind pre-flop, and last outright on all subsequent rounds – in effect, then, the button gets to see what everyone else does before making a decision, which is a key advantage.

This means if you're the button, you have a number of options of which everyone else should be wary, and such an advantage is just as important as the cards you're holding and understanding the other players you're up against. Particularly in no-limit or pot-limit games, it means you're in prime position for bluffing, as if no one else gets involved, you can attack the blinds, or re-raise players who appear weak.

In poker, you need a better hand to call with than to raise with, and on the button you can often force other players to fold pre-flop, particularly since they know you have this last option on three more betting rounds, by the end of which the pot could be absolutely huge. Moreover, when they do call, you just need to bear in mind that a player who checks you will often be weak, so you don't even have to have a pair to try to move them off the hand.

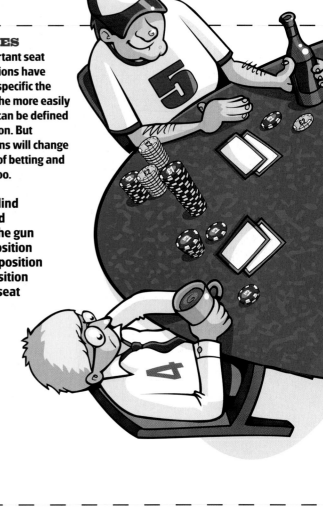

PLACE NAMES
In poker, the important seat placings and positions have names. The more specific the name a seat has, the more easily the player's hand can be defined according to position. But remember, positions will change after every round of betting and after every hand too.

1	Small blind
2	Big blind
3	Under the gun
3-4	Early position
5-6	Middle position
7-9	Late position
8	Cut-off seat
9	Button

> The best policy if you're under the gun is to accept your limitations and pass anything that doesn't look rock-solid against a full table

At the other end of the scale, being under the gun is the worst position, as you have to act first pre-flop when your opponents are trying to spot exactly how strong you are, and then early on in subsequent rounds if you continue in the hand. If you raise with anything less than a great hand, someone else might re-raise or call and try to trap you, and if you just call, you have lots of players behind who might raise and make playing more expensive.

The best policy in this position is always to accept your limitations and pass anything that doesn't look rock-solid against a full table. What this translates to depends on the game and the other players – for example, in tough limit games, a first-position raise might only mean A-A, K-K or A-K, and A-J or 8-8 might be hands to throw away, whereas in no limit, your implied odds and the element of deception mean you might raise with 8♥-9♥ or A-Q and call with a variety of hands. This last option depends on how aggressive your opponents are, whether

you're likely to see some cheap flops, and whether they're going to make you pay for being out of position later on with some heavy betting.

Straight down the middle

In middle position, you have a mixture of factors working for and against you, and pragmatism is often the most sensible option. If no one acts first, you might raise in order to isolate the blinds, and continue playing aggressively if you 'win' the button by forcing everyone before it to fold and are only up against one or both blinds (who may just be calling as they already have some money in the hand).

Alternatively, if early-position players raise or those behind you call or re-raise, you might want to fold pre-flop or at least play more cautiously afterwards. Anyone can get dealt a great hand, and your main advantage with position is being one step ahead in guessing what they have and being able to exert some pressure if they show weakness. If you don't like the information you're getting before the action comes to you, or if an opponent seems unconcerned by the

pressure you're trying to apply, it's usually best to back off a little and even consider folding to a bet. You shouldn't get carried away if you find yourself pushing against a brick wall. Below are some scenarios using our nine-handed paradigm:

SCENARIO 1 A BASIC NICK?

No-limit hold'em tournament, mid stages – Everyone folds around to the button who raises as usual to three times the big blind. Both blinds, who are tight and passive players, fold. Did the big blind have a hand? Maybe, but on the other hand maybe not… A classic late-position play to keep yourself afloat mid-tournament, especially if there are antes in place.

SCENARIO 2 GET OUT OF THE WAY!

NLH tournament, early stages – A tight player raises under the gun to 3 BB, all pass around to the small blind who re-raises to 10 BB. Then the big blind goes all-in. Forget position, everyone here has been dealt great cards, but who has the Aces? ➤

SCENARIO 3 YOUTHFUL CUNNING, OR YOUTHFUL EXUBERANCE?

Pot-limit hold'em tournie, mid to late stages – Under the gun calls, a mid-position player raises the pot and another player calls. All fold back to under the gun, who now re-raises the pot. What should the other players do with good but not great hands here? Traditionally, most players would only check-raise in early position with Aces in order to get some money in the pot or trap someone. Nowadays, though, the new brand of aggressive player – and a few inexperienced ones – are lowering the bar and either trying to make this super-strength play with lesser hands (maybe A-K or J-J) to get it all-in or force others to fold. Or they decide that if they can't see a cheap flop, they'd rather lump it all in with a hand such as 9-9 than face a tricky one out of position. A few enthusiastic souls have even been seen making extravagant versions of this play in NLH tournaments with holdings such as 7-3 OS.

SCENARIO 4 CRITICAL MASS OR PLAYING FOR LAUGHS?

Limit hold'em, cash – All pass to the cut-off seat, who raises and is called only by the big blind. The big blind checks the flop and the cut-off player bets. What have you learned about their hands? Well, this depends on the stakes and the players, but in many instances you'll have gleaned nothing, although you've learned a valuable lesson in positional limit hold'em play.

A late-position player will often raise with a variety of hands to steal or isolate, and the big blind who is getting 7/2 on their money will often call to look at the flop. If they check it, the other player will bet 90% or more of the time, as they might win the pot there or at least make the big blind check the turn, offering the aggressor the chance of a free card on the more expensive round of betting. Because of the nondescript nature of the betting amounts, the raiser could have Aces or junk, and you'd have little to go on in the big blind. As such, the scare factor is high, as you could get drawn into calling a series of bets.

Generally speaking, in low-limit games (under $5 or $10), play is much looser and softer, so players might bet, call and bluff here with anything. In mid-limit games ($5/ $10-$50/$100), players may be much tighter and tougher and continue less. In high-limit games where each bet is massive ($50-$100 upwards), the players often employ an ultra-aggressive strategy to confuse their opponents.

SCENARIO 5 THE TURN CHECK-RAISE

NLH tournament, early stages – Mid-position, solid-aggressive player makes a standard raise, which is called by the button and the big blind. On a flop of Q, J, 7, the blind checks, the aggressive player bets as might be expected, the button folds and the blind calls. The turn comes a blank and, again, it goes check/bet, but then the blind re-raises all-in, after which the aggressive player thinks for a while and folds, grumbling about his luck.

What did they have? Almost certainly, the blind had a good or great hand, maybe 7-7 or J-Q, or had read the other guy for nothing, and the raiser might have had anything from A-Q to a bluff (depending on his level of respect for the blind) and either surrendered the bluff or made a big laydown, feeling like he was trapped. The turn check-raise has

this power, as it usually gets most of the money in the pot and doesn't often mean a draw. As such, a hand's odds of completing drop massively from flop to turn.

SCENARIO 6 A FLOP STORY...

PLH, cash – Most live cash games in the UK are played pot limit and with deep stacks, meaning several rounds of betting. As such, positional play is key, as your opponents can put all of your money in jeopardy by the end of the hand or make tricky check-raises. With blinds of £1 or £2, Tony raises the pot to £7 under the gun and gets three callers before the blinds, of whom the big blind calls the extra £5. This isn't unusual: even if Tony has Aces, the others have enough money on the table to call in late position and try to trap him.

The flop comes 7♥, 6♥, 2♦, the big blind checks and Tony bets out £30 into the £36 pot, suggesting strength but not offering the others an open invitation to call or fold. Seat five folds, Ben in seat six calls, then David in seat seven calls and raises the pot to the maximum £126. The big blind folds. Tony calls the extra, as does Ben. The turn is the 9♠ and Tony checks as does Ben, then David bets all-in £250 into a pot of £504, Tony thinks and raises all-in and Ben calls all-in another £460. The river is a blank and Tony shakes his head, preparing to muck, and flashes Q-Q to his neighbour. David reveals 7-7 and Ben turns over 8♥-10♥ for the nuts.

Tony had decided to bet out with a good but not unassailable hand in early position and try to force it through against what could have been a flush draw and slightly lower pair, only to find position his ever-increasing enemy. Ben had called pre-flop and on the flop, as he was getting decent odds with the suited connectors, and then the flush and straight draw against what looked like over-pairs or trips. David had 7-7 and tried to hit his set (as he did) and use position to drive the others out on a dangerous flop, where he had the best. Ultimately, though, he fell victim to the monster he helped create. So Ben won a huge pot by playing it cute with an off-beat hand in the middle of two second-best hands that both thought they were ahead because of their position. ❆

> In middle position, you have a mixture of factors working both for and against you, and pragmatism is often the most sensible option

Size
DOES MATTER

There's no doubt about it: when it comes to your stack, bigger is better. But what can you do when you're not so well endowed (with chips)? **Roland de Wolfe** reveals the strategies for tournament hold'em that could help you get out of a hole when short-stacked, and also how to squash the opposition when you're chip leader

There are certain players who you can destroy at a poker table but you will never have more chips than them. Oil magnates, self-made billionaires, poker writers... If you play cash games with these types, you might be able to decimate their stack but they will re-buy in an instant without a second thought.

Even in a cash game at your local casino there will be players with bankrolls that are huge in relation to the size of the game. While these people and their continual re-buying may be good for your bank balance, you will never be in a position where your chip stack dominates them.

Tournament play, however, is a very different kettle of fish. In tournaments, the worth of a man's play can truly be measured by the size of his stack. But, to coin a phrase, while bigger is undoubtedly better, it's not necessarily the size of your stack that matters, but what you do with it.

In tournaments, players will find themselves in situations to which they are unaccustomed. Sometimes, you will find yourself the chip leader, on other occasions you will be chip dog. In these two situations, the same hand must often be played very differently.

BIG STACK

When you have a big stack, people take notice. Opponents are much less likely to steal your blind or raise into you. That's because in tournaments, once you lose your chips, you are history. One of the most basic rules is not to get involved with the chip leader unless you have to.

Much of what you do, as ever in hold'em, will be dictated by position. When you are in early position (for instance, first, second or third to act in a nine-handed game) you need a genuine hand to raise. Even if you are a massive chip leader, you don't want to risk losing your chips to people behind you. If you are on a slow clock (the blinds only go up infrequently), much of the play will take place at the final table and although your chip lead is important, you will not win the tournament when there is more than one table left. So from an early position you must have a premium hand.

You should avoid regularly playing medium suited connectors, such as 6♣-7♣ or 9♥-10♥. The reason for this is that in no-limit or pot-limit, after a couple of hours of play, the blinds will be big enough that you will be unable to call a significant-sized raise. If you do look down to find A-K, Q-Q, K-K or A-A then it is better to raise. It is

unlikely, if you're the big stack that you will get re-raised. Therefore, you are likely to face two or three players and will be an underdog to win the pot, whereas if you only have one caller, you will be favourite, unless he has a higher pair.

In mid-position (fourth, fifth or sixth to act in a nine-handed game) you can be slightly bolder than in early position. If you are sixth to act, you may think about stealing the two blinds. This is an advantage of having the big stack. As in late position, it depends who is to act after you. If they are rocks who will fold if anyone raises them when they don't have a premium hand, then it is worth exploiting when you have a passable hand.

You would not want to raise with 9-4 off-suit, but you could raise with A-9 suited or J-10 suited because – unless you run into a monster hand like Kings or Aces – you will see a flop and have a chance of flopping at least a draw. You can try and see more flops in mid-position when you have a big stack. Even if it's just the big blind and yourself who see the flop, it may be worth a bet if your hand has not improved. That is because even if the big blind has bottom or middle pair they may not call a raise and risk getting into a battle with the big stack.

Conversely, if you do have a premium hand, you may only want to call a raise or make a small bet into an unraised pot. If you have Aces, your big stack will certainly scare off A-10 or A-J with a re-raise. It may be better for them in this instance to hit their 10 or A and think they have the best of it, thus handily enabling you to extract some more chips out of them.

Leave it till late

It is in late position that being the biggest stack is most advantageous. Playing on the button at all but the most aggressive players, you should try to steal their blinds irrespective of your cards. You should not even have to look at your cards!

Your opponents will really need to have a hand to enter a flop with the chip leader. If they have a monster, they will re-raise and you can put it down, but if they have a fair hand such as A-10 or 9-9 and don't hit their flop, you can find this out with one bet and may well take a larger pot than if you had not raised it. You can also do this from one off the button or in the small and big blind. The exception is when facing a small stack as they may be forced to call to avoid being blinded away.

> When you have a big stack, people take notice. In tournaments, one of the most basic rules is not to get involved with the chip leader

SHOOTOUT TOURNAMENT STRATEGY

Image is everything in this ever-more popular poker variant

Shootout tournaments are becoming increasingly popular – TV tournaments are often in this format – and the strategy to take in these is different to multi-table tournaments. You play a single table of around ten people and have to win or come second in that table. Most of the play is later on in these events when the blinds are high.

Early on, it does not matter whether you gain or lose 20% of your stack. Building table image is far more important. If it is a qualifying heat and the aim is only to finish in the top

one or two, it is much better to play conservatively at the start and save confrontation until the later stages. By that time, your table image of being a tight player should let you steal blinds that are actually worth something.

If you do get chips early, in the first few levels, then hold on to them. If, however, you find yourself short then be patient. It is when it goes three- or four-handed that the play will decide who gets the spoils. Before then it is just not worth risking chips.

Don't be one-dimensional

Even when you're more heavily stacked than Dolly Parton, it is important to vary your play. If you keep raising, all but the weakest players will twig and start playing back at you. You want to take your fair share of blinds from late position, but don't want to be in every pot. Even in late position it is not advisable to continually be calling with A-Q or Q-J suited or any hand where if you hit you can still do your dough. You also don't need to be in the 50/50 pots.

Avoid calling when you think you are facing two overcards to your smaller pair or vice versa. You can raise with these hands, but you don't need to call as you don't need be in these gambling hands when you are chip leader. Be aggressive but don't be wild or have a laissez faire attitude to your chips. You may be doing well, very well, but the real money in most tournaments does not start until the final table, so you are not moving up the money ladder by gaining chips at this stage, just gaining a stronger foothold on it.

Work on your reputation. If you have become chip leader by playing solid, then loosen up – people will respect your raises. If you have got there through loose play and playing non-premium starting hands then tighten up; only play when you are favourite and you will be paid out on your hands.

SHORT STACK

The people with the most chips know that ultimately their main obstacles to the big stack will be the fellow chip monsters first at their table and then in the tournament as a whole. Often, though, the big stacks will try and

> **Even when you're more heavily stacked than Dolly Parton, you must vary your play. If you keep raising, all but the weakest players will play back at you**

delay confrontation with each other. Instead, they gang up on the smaller-stacked players to try and eliminate them and move themselves closer to a guaranteed money finish.

The best way to play the small stack often depends on just how small you are. If you are really small and cannot survive more than one more round of blinds then, when you get a passable hand, you have to go all-in, whatever position you're playing. If you find yourself in the big blind and the compulsory posting is half your stack, then you are pot committed and have little alternative but to go all-in. You will not survive another round of blinds and even if you do double up, you will only be in the same position again one round later. It is true tournaments are about survival, but there is no point being blinded away.

Whatever two cards you have are unlikely to be that much of an underdog against any other two cards. Under different circumstances you may have mucked the hand you go all in with but remember that 8-5 is less than a 2/1 underdog against A-K.

Short but not *that* short

If your stack is short but not dire then you have far more options. Playing in early position, you have to be even more careful what you raise with, as big stacks will be more likely to call you. If there are two of them on your table then they may put you all in and then not bet against each other, to try and eliminate you. If you have Aces or Kings then you will probably be happy to take your chances, but if you are holding A-K or Q-Q, you may want to see a flop before committing all your chips.

In mid-position and facing only one big stack, you may want to raise with any Ace with Jack kicker or better and a pair of Jacks or higher. If you are unlucky enough to run into something higher then you will need an outdraw, but you may be getting your hand in with the best of it in a two-way pot or win the hand uncontested.

In late position, you will need a lot less to raise the pot. It is not advisable to try and steal the blinds from someone who is chipped up. They may call with less as they can afford to see a flop and may have the added bonus of decimating your stack and knocking you out. If you do want to nick the blinds, it is not worth doing so from a fellow short stack as they too are unlikely to pass even a hand as weak as one high card or anything suited.

It is the medium-sized stacks whose blinds are up for grabs. They will probably give you more respect if you are short stacked as they will reckon you have a lot to lose and would not want to risk tournament exit. Again, whether you want to attempt to take the blinds from the button or one off the button may depend on whether you think you will be called. If the blinds are rocks it may be worth trying to steal, but if they are loose or have been prone to defending their blind, it may be unwise, unless you are sure you will call a re-raise.

Some players may try to hang in there for as long as possible, but this is only the best strategy if you are near (or in) the tournament prize money and there are other short-stacked players. Being short stacked not only makes you a target for others, it bars you from many important aspects of a successful game such as seeing flops, playing drawing hands and picking up the blinds. It is vital to get out of the position as soon as possible. ✿

SUGGESTED PLAYS

This is a table of situations where you should play it differently due to the size of your stack. These are not definitive plays but are the ones that should be used most frequently.

HAND	POSITION	POT	SHORT STACK	BIG STACK
A-K OS	Early	Unraised	Call	Raise
A-8 S	Mid	Unraised	Fold	Call
Q-Q	Mid	Raised	Re-raise	Call
Q-9 S	Late	Unraised	Call/raise	Raise
8-7 S	Late	Raised	Fold	Call

KEY OS off-suit **S** suited

IT'S PLAY TIME

Get ready for some serious, big-money action!
Tournaments can be a brilliant way to make your
name – and your fortune

Poker players tend to be divided into two camps: those who play in cash games and those who prefer to compete in tournaments. This division is reflected in online play, where you can play in cash or 'ring' games, or tournaments.

Oddly, some of the world's greatest players such as Phil Hellmuth, who has won nine World Series of Poker bracelets, are relatively poor cash-game players and so avoid playing in them. However, the very best pros, such as Daniel Negreanu, are superb at both forms of play.

On the whole, though, players want to become established at tournament play, and the best way to get good at this is to take part in the hundreds of tournaments that take place online every day. And what a choice there is! You can play in one-table 'tournies' (known as sit'n'gos), in which you play against nine others and the first three split the prize money, usually on a 50%-30%-20% basis. Or you can play in multi-table tournaments, where you could find yourself competing against more than 2,000 other online players. It will take several hours to get to the final table and the prize money, even for a $10 buy-in, will be considerable.

Whichever tournament you choose to play in, you'll find there are certain strategies you need to adopt to survive and succeed, and so we address these in this section.

You'll find an essential guide to how to play 'rebuy' tournies, in which players can rebuy chips as may times as they like for the first period of play if they get busted out early. After that, the play then moves to the 'freeze-out' phase, during which you can't rebuy and if you're busted out, you're out for good. It's essential to modify the way you play in this phase of a tournament and in actual freeze-out tournaments, too.

You'll also find out how to perfect your game when playing 'heads-up' – that is, when you're in a tournament and it's just you and one other player left. This is often the weakest part of a player's game, so learning how to be an effective heads-up player adds a very big weapon to your poker armoury.

The *fast* and the FURIOUS

They offer good odds of making money and are so fast you're in and out within the hour. Sit&go poker tournaments are all the rage online, so **Phil Shaw** explains how to cash in on the one-table tournament boom

S it&gos, or mini-tournaments, are fast becoming one of the most popular online poker formats. To join in, all you have to do is sign up at the level of your choosing (anything from $1 up to $1,000), and then wait for the other seats to fill and you're off! They come in varying sizes, the traditional format being nine or ten player games where the top three get paid on a 50%-30%-20% structure.

You'll find thousands of players at an average site. You can get some valuable experience so that when you make a big final table, you'll already have an idea of how to play. ➤

SIT, PLAY, LOSE – AND GO

James Hipwell is a sit&go tournament regular. Here he describes what to expect at a typical event

I have to confess to already being a bit of a sit&go nut. I usually play in a few of these a week, usually in the $30 buy-ins, and have made good money from them in the six months since I started playing online poker. It's in the ring games that I tend to get badly burned. Then again, I am a bit of a fish!

Today I decide to go a bit low-rent and play in a measly $5 no-limit Texas hold'em game so I log on *vcpoker.com* and go to the one-table tournament part of the site. There's a $5 game that is filling up pretty quick so I join the table and collect my $1,500 of chips.

I play under the name Slicker66 (don't ask) and today I'm up against a few names I know I've done battle with before: there's cowboywombat, Boarderz88, bobbybobby, danuts777 (must fancy himself a bit, this bloke), mm88, thevillian (can't he spell villain?), ukdon, dragondog2 (what the..?) and VicktheViking. A tough-sounding lot.

The game starts and I'm in the big blind with K-6 OS. mm88 raises to $125 which I think is a bit toppy so I fold. This guy's a bit loose, I reckon.

On the second hand that's confirmed when mm88 goes all-in with bugger-all and is called by thevillian with pocket cowboys (K-S). He gets them busted and is out of the tournie after 90 seconds when outdrawn with a vastly

> These games are fast and furious with the chip-leader changing seemingly every hand

superior hand. What a fish this mm guy is!

That's the beauty of these single-table tournies – they're fast and furious with the chip-leader changing seemingly every hand. At the moment I'm just not hitting any cards and am getting bossed out of pots, and losing my blinds, by the guys with the big stacks. That's dragondog2, ViktheViking and cowboywombat, who seems even more loose-aggressive than mm88.

After 25 minutes I'm down to $625 from my original $1,500 and am in need of something, *anything*, to go all-in with. It comes when I'm dealt K-Q OS and I raise all-in pre-flop. Everyone folds and I get no action but with the blinds now up at $75-$150 I add $225 to my stack.

Going all-in

A few hands later I'm dealt pocket sevens, which isn't great but with the cards I'm getting I reckon it's about the best hand I'm gonna get before the blinds wipe me out. So I'm on my feet again and raise all-in. I'm called by cowboywombat with A-K, so it's a coin-flip. I'm still ahead after the flop but a dreaded Ace appears on the turn and I'm out of the tournament. It's been fun, I'm $5 down but I'll get it back tonight in a $30 game, won't I?

> Sit&gos are also great if you're aspiring to be a serious player as they offer a reliable return, which is good news for your bankroll (20-30 buy-ins is plenty to keep you safe) plus the opportunity to play short-handed against players who might not have the requisite skills.

So, without further ado, let's look at the best ways to make money from sit&go tournaments. Here, we examine how to play short, medium and large stacks in the stages up to the money positions and how things change when you get there…

Short stack play

Every tournament has a beginning, middle and end. However, the middle in a sit&go is shorter than in a big event, and even if you don't get off to a great start and end up short stacked, your chances of scraping into third or even second are still considerable. For this reason, if your efforts in the early stages come to nothing, you need to do your utmost to preserve a decent portion of your starting chips (at least two-thirds) to make use of in the 'squeeze-out' middle stage of the game. This is where there are four or five players remaining and the blinds are high enough to be worth stealing with all-ins. Other players will need far better hands than in a cash game to call you, as long as you're in a position to do their stack some damage and put them in danger of missing out on the money, that is.

For this reason, tighter-than-normal play is recommended in the early stages. However, if you're on a very slow structure, you can still play some speculative hands, such as small pairs or suited connectors, in the hope of winning a very big pot. If you get out in front, you can then start to open up your game a bit and pick spots to pressurise short-stacked opponents. If you don't get in front, you can tighten up and still go into the squeeze-out stage with a chance of either building back up, or doubling through into a better position than the one in which you started.

Once you get into the squeeze-out stage, a lot of what happens next depends how fast the blinds go up. On a slow structure, the last four can thrust and parry for a long time until someone makes a fatal mistake or two big hands collide. If the blinds quickly

Sit&gos are great if you're aspiring to be a serious player as they offer a reliable return, which is good for your bankroll

Table	Type	Stakes	Avg Pot	Plrs
Twister	Lim	$150/$300	915	0
National Treasure	Lim	$50/$100	350	0
The Great Caruso	Lim	$20/$40	82	0
The Third Man (6 player max)	Lim	$20/$40	128	0
Network	NL	$10/$20	88	0
Help!	Lim	$10/$20	78	7
Anna and the King (6 player max)	Lim	$10/$20	51	2
The Last Picture Show	Lim	$10/$20	92	0
Apocalypse Now (6 player max)	NL	$5/$10	23	4
Seabiscuit	NL	$5/$10	50	0
April Love	Lim	$5/$10	68	9
Splendor in the Grass (6 player max)	Lim	$5/$10	45	6
Inherit The Wind (6 player max)	Lim	$5/$10	47	0
Brazil	Lim	$5/$10	40	0
Tokyo	Lim	$4/$8	21	2
Vertigo (6 player max)	Lim	$4/$8	30	0
M*A*S*H	NL	$3/$6	187	9
Catch 22 (6 player max)	NL	$3/$6	128	6

VC POKER'S LOBBY You'll never have any trouble finding plenty of action when you play online with VC Poker

get astronomical, though, people will be forced to go all-in and call with far less. Again, this is a complex situation to be in, and requires you to be highly adaptable to changing circumstances in the game.

For example, on a slow structure, you're less likely to be worried about being anted away with a short stack than falling out of contention compared with your opponents. In this case, you should wait for good opportunities to get involved and at least partly base your decisions as to when to go all-in on the relation of your chip stack to that of the next lowest player. Try not to fall more than 50% behind them and attack them at every favourable moment in an effort to sneak into third position so they're then the one under the most pressure.

However, on a fast structure, it may simply come down to a matter of counting how many hands you can survive until the blinds eat you up, and looking for the best hand and situation to go all-in. Either way, though, you need to stay with the pace in order to pose a realistic threat.

Medium- and big-stack play

Now let's assume you've played well in the early stages – not taken too many undue risks and won a few nice pots with speculative hands – and have arrived in the middle stages with an average stack for the last four or five players. Now what? Well, the bad news it that your work is still far from done, as you can easily leave empty handed. Looking on the bright side, though, you're in no immediate danger unless of course you do something silly or get short.

The first thing to do in this situation is to look around you and see what the other players have in front of them. For example, in a game with very short and big stacks, you might expect some fireworks, with the big stacks trying to bully and the shorter ones trying to double through or steal the blinds. On the other hand, if everyone has the same, there's likely to be a delicate equilibrium that no one wants to disturb for fear of becoming the whipping boy (of course, the blinds and players play a big part in how long this lasts).

As such, when there are different-sized stacks, if there's only one short stack between you and the money, you

should try to stay out of harm's way as much as possible (unless a great hand comes along) until things change one way or another. However, if the stacks are pretty evenly matched, you need to carefully look for ways to maintain your chips or get ahead without risking a disaster, as any all-in benefits the bystanding players so much.

So by extension, then, as risking an exit at this stage is such a disaster for a player, if you get a really big stack (approaching 50% of the chips in play), you can really start to use it against those who have some kind of understanding of short- and medium-stack survival tactics by playing very aggressively against them. Frequently raise their blinds; reraise them all-in when there's another, shorter stack still to go from the last four and they have enough chips to pass; or bluff a lot after the flop. You shouldn't risk a lot more chips with a marginal hand if another player shows commitment, but remember this is a chance to effectively win the game there and then by getting a mile in front. Even if you do lose an all-in, you have probably paid for it with all the small pots you've stolen. What's more, the other players will know you're gunning for them and won't pass easily next time.

Down to the last three

When you get to the last three, the blinds will probably be quite high and, after the tension of the squeeze-out stage, the players will loosen up considerably. If you were the big stack, remember your bullying privileges have just been revoked to a large extent. If, however, you were the short or medium ones, this is the time to gamble it up!

> **If everyone has the same, there's likely to be a delicate equilibrium that no one wants to disturb for fear of becoming the whipping boy**

Assuming the traditional 50/30/20 structure, the smallest change in pay by position is from third to second, so it's well worth taking on the bigger stacks at the first decent opportunity in the hope of being in contention for first position (although if there's one very short stack, you might still wait for them to go).

If you have fewer than ten big blinds and find a decent hand, you might as well go all-in (unless it's a real monster and you want action), as you have nothing to lose. Similarly, if you're the big stack with any kind of a hand, you might as well force the short stack to commit. Because of this situation and the pace of a three-handed game, you will probably reach heads-up play quite soon after making the money. However, that's another story entirely.

Trading up

Sit&go tournaments are great fun and are usually wrapped up within an hour, so good if you're in a hurry. They are a good way to improve your strategy and can also be extremely remunerative once you get good at them.

The best way to start is to play in the dirt-cheap $5 games (see our box on the previous page for further information on how they work) where you will find plenty of loose-aggressive action. Then, as you improve your game and your confidence grows you can 'trade up' to the $50 and even $100 tournaments. The way the pay-out structure usually works means that if you win a $50 game your first prize would amount to a healthy $250, which is not be be sniffed at.

But be warned: once you go beyond the magic $100 level you're most definitely in the 'pro' camp and up against some of the finest poker brains on the planet. So keep your wits about you, remember all you've learned so far and sit&go for it! ❈

Extra lives when the kitty dies

Playing like a maniac and going all-in regularly means certain death in normal poker. Not so with rebuys.
Phil Shaw shows how buying back in when your stack is low can keep you out of the poker cemetery

Most people are familiar with the concept of poker tournaments by now, thanks to the internet and televised poker, whether it's the $10,000 main event at the World Series of Poker or a $10 event on any of hundreds of sites. Most of these are 'freezeouts' – that is, you're eliminated as soon as you lose your chips (even if this happens on the very first hand), but there's

also a completely different type of possibility on offer in most places – the 'rebuy tournament'.

In these events, there's a designated 'rebuy period' (usually the first hour), during which you can buy more chips if you go broke. Depending on the specific rules, you can do this as many times as you want when you have chips but fall below a certain level (or even straight away). Sometimes you

can also take an 'add-on' at the end of the rebuy period, whereby you can buy even more chips irrespective of how many you have accumulated.

Because of this, strategy during this part of a tournament is radically different to the freezeout stage of the event – that is, when the rebuy period is over – or a straight freezeout. In short, you need to have a few rebuys in your pocket, a good gambling attitude and the ability to see exactly who is playing what game during this stage, as well as how their game alters afterwards.

So rebuy events sound right up your street, eh? Great, but hang on a second, as there are a few things you need to take into consideration before you even play a hand if you want to make them profitable.

Get stacked

First, you need to check the rules and structures to ensure your pockets are deep enough and to determine your overall strategy. For example, in a $10 online rebuy event, you might need to budget around $50, as some sites not only offer add-ons, but allow you to rebuy before the first hand – basically, whenever you have the usual amount of starting chips or less. Moreover, with often-huge fields online, it's normally a good idea to buy more chips whenever you're given the opportunity so you can build a stack and have an advantage over players who don't have one.

You may also go broke at some stage and need to rebuy this 'double stack', although doing so more than once probably isn't advisable. With two double buy-ins of $20 and an add-on of $10, $50 is a good ballpark figure to keep in mind. However, if only single buy-ins are allowed, $30 would be pretty reasonable.

This strategy usually holds true, but you also need to check on how many chips you get at which stages for your money. For example, buy-ins and rebuys are usually the same amount of chips, but some events might give more for the add-on as an extra incentive to take it.

This can represent a significant difference – for example, if a site offers double buy-ins where you get 1,500 chips for $10 (so 3,000 for $20 to start with) and an add-on of 2,000 chips for $10, you should probably just play as normal and gamble it up. Conversely, if you're only allowed single buy-ins of 1,000 chips for $10, but an add-on where you get 2,000 chips for another $10, it's probably more correct to play extremely tight and ensure you don't need to take unnecessary rebuys where you only get the 1,000 chips. For the purposes of this article, though, we'll assume the latter isn't the case, as all you need to do there is fold unless you find a monster or flop a big hand cheaply!

Unlike in a freezeout, where people usually play very tight in the early levels while trying to figure each other

out, it's common to see several people go all-in on the first hand of a small buy-in rebuy event and turn over hands such as 4-4, K-7 and A-2! This is great news if you're on their table, as you've found some real gamblers and, if you play it right, you could be sitting on a mountain of chips by the end of the rebuy period for only a small outlay.

Just ask yourself this: if one table has 40 rebuys on it and another has only ten, then which table is more likely to produce the eventual winner? For this reason, you need to do as much as possible to encourage the gambling spirit while keeping things as cheap as possible for yourself. This might mean talking it up with the maniacs and making a few inexpensive raises or bluffs (which, of course, you can show to loosen everyone up), going all-in a few times, or just generally giving the impression that you're there to gamble.

Of course, this isn't exactly the case, as there's no point ending up with 20,000 in chips if that's what they would have cost you if you were able to buy them. Rather, you want to create the illusion of being a maniac – as poker legend Doyle Brunson wrote: 'you have to give action to get action' – and this is particularly true in rebuy events, as people are far less likely to gamble with a rock.

This is easy enough to do, as since most rebuy events are pot limit or no limit and the sizes of bets tend to get exponentially bigger through the betting rounds, you can make a lot of 'advertising' raises and bluffs before the flop or on it without denting your stack. However, because of them, people will frequently mis-categorise you and pay you off when you have a hand and make big bets on the turn and river, or go all-in before the flop with a big hand.

Success or disaster?

If there's one certainty about this approach it's that the volatility of your results in the rebuy period can go through the roof as you're gambling so much and often playing far more hands than you would normally. As such, as things progress, you're probably either going to end up accumulating a big stack or going broke, and when this happens you need to consider whether it's time to change strategy.

For example, if you sit down and more than double your starting chips in the first half of the rebuy period, you might want to tighten up a bit, as your plan has been successful and you don't really want to get low again. Besides, if you do make this decision, the chances are the other players won't notice for a while anyway, and so if you do pick up some big hands, you're just as likely to get paid with them.

However, if you go broke and decide to take a rebuy, you need to start thinking about how much you're prepared to spend, or if you want to continue at all.

For example, if this happens very early in the game and the table is a good one, you might be happy to go over budget in order to keep to the gambling style. On the other hand, if you're at a poor or tough table or the rebuy period is nearly over, you might just decide to tighten up and wait for the freezeout stage, or even give up and leave if you go broke again – after all, if others have a massive stack already, then you're going to be at a huge disadvantage anyway.

The big freeze(out)...

The freezeout stages of a rebuy event throw up a few special circumstances. Most importantly, you need to observe how people's styles change compared with how they played during the rebuy period – for example, have they noticed at all that a change of strategy is needed, have they taken add-ons or extra rebuys if these were available to them, and how many chips do they now have compared with the blinds and average stacks (both at your table and overall)?

Consider these points as you enter the freezeout stage of the tournament (and mentally compare them to other events you've played) and you'll be well on the way to the final table.

> You need to encourage the gambling spirit, while keeping things as cheap as possible for yourself

THE COLD LIGHT OF PLAY

Ever kicked yourself for getting carried away in the heat of the moment during the freezeout section of a poker tournament? Follow **Phil Shaw's** advice and you'll have a better chance of raking in those monster pots

Many people have tasted the thrill of poker tournaments by now, either on TV as a spectator or first-hand on the internet, where the biggest weekly events offer first prizes of over $100,000. But what, other than the money, is it that makes them so much fun and so interesting? Besides the lure of a fixed liability, they also require some quite specialist knowledge that can give you a significant edge over the field. Read on, and we hope to let you in on a few trade secrets…

'Freezeout' tournaments are when you can't buy more chips if you lose the ones you have, and either start in this format or revert to it after a 'rebuy period' where you can buy more chips for a set amount of time. Both formats play largely the same, but if there's been a rebuy period then some of the concepts in our 'Chips change value' boxout (see page 69) will come into play immediately, whereas if everyone starts with the same amount this will take a while to have any effect.

Weathering the cold front

You will be paid according to where you finish as people are eliminated, and so your motives are first to survive and then to thrive!

Whether it's the start of a freezeout proper or the rebuy period has just finished, the opening rounds of most events are going to be quite cagey affairs with people feeling each other out and seeing how the table plays. The blinds will be very low at this stage compared to the average stack (perhaps 50 to 100 big blinds) and so big pots and all-ins will be rare, and similarly there will be plenty of flops and play through the rounds.

Because of these circumstances, there couldn't be a better time to try to get in a few pots with hands like suited connectors or small pairs that could win you decent amounts for a relatively small outlay, and conversely you will need to make healthy raises to protect your big hands from all the jackals out there who are looking for a sign of weakness.

CHIPS CHANGE VALUE
SO DON'T GET LEFT OUT IN THE COLD

Beware: failure to understand how chip values vary in a freezeout tournie from a cash game could cost you dear

One of the hardest thing for newcomers to tournament poker to get to grips with is how the value of tournament chips is different to those in the cash games everyone is familiar with.

When Greg Raymer won the ultimate freezeout – the World Series of Poker – last year he walked away with a cool $5,000,000, but he actually had over $25,000,000 of chips in front of him when it was all over. The difference had, of course, gone to the other people who had placed in the event, which perhaps illustrates why winning a tournament can jokingly be referred to as a bad beat in itself...

By contrast, if you make it into the money with only one chip left, that chip is worth much more than its cash value. Similarly, everyone is familiar with the phrase 'a chip and a chair', illustrated well by a famous story from the 1982 World Series.

From tiny chips are fortunes grown

Jack 'Treetops' Strauss moved in what he thought was his whole stack only to be called and lose. But then as he was preparing to leave he found a chip concealed under a kink in the felt, from which he came back to win the entire event!

In short then, because tournament players are paid by position the more chips you have the less they are worth individually, and the fewer you have the more they are worth.

What this means in practice is that it's actually correct to play very aggressively with a big stack to bully those players who are worried about getting knocked out (while you can't be damaged too much), and to play extremely tightly with a short stack as your next hand could be the last and you want to find something good to make a stand with.

Between these then are the middle stacks, who need to balance their play depending on what stack sizes they face, and try to build rather than be knocked down.

If you watch a tournament closely, you'll be able to see these factors at work without much effort, and you'll have learnt one of the principal dynamics of poker tournaments – good players play according to their stack size, as chips mean power!

Of course, you could adopt more extreme strategies in both directions, and either play very tight in the beginning in the hope of 'turning the tables' later or play super-aggressively to try and get some chips and force the opposition to back off while the pressure is still minimal (see our box on page 70). Whatever your strategy, your aim is to get some chips, and so you might need to tailor it to the table you're at and the quality of the hands you're getting.

It's the ideal time to try to get in a few pots with hands like suited connectors or small pairs that can win you big amounts for little outlay

As the blinds start to rise and different sized stacks begin to emerge, the average stack drops to maybe 20-30 big blinds and the game usually starts to change character – becoming much tighter and more aggressive, with bigger hands rising in value and drawing hands becoming less worth investing in, and considerably fewer flops being seen as pots revert to the 'raise and take it', or 'raise and re-raise' paradigm.

Skating on thin ice

Unlike a sit&go though, where the money is close and the game increasingly short-handed at this point, in a freezeout tournie you're often still hours away from getting paid and every time someone is eliminated another player takes their place.

What this means then is that it's time to dig in, and unless you have a big stack to wreak havoc with, you're going to need to exercise a bit of caution on the basis that every hand you play could easily be your last!

Tables will normally be nine- or ten-handed right the way down to the money and this means that you will probably find ➤

TURNING THE TABLES
WHEN STACK SIZE REALLY DOES MATTER

It's all fine and well managing your own stack well in a freezeout tournament, but you'll need to keep an eye on the rest of the table too

When you watch an event on TV or the internet, you'll have seen how stack size affects the way people play – but what about when you're in the thick of it and trying to work your way to the final table without any major setbacks? Well, you know how to play according to your stack now, but what about how the rest of the table affects your strategy?

Questions you need answers to are: How does the rest of the table perceive you? Where are the big stacks and the aggressive players at the table? How do the stacks compare to the blinds and averages? Are you close to the money? Is anyone actively exploiting the stack-size factor in the same way you hope to?

If you start thinking about these issues you'll gain much more insight into what's going on than if you approached the game on its own. For example, if you've played tight early on then people will try to bully you more, but respect your raises and not move against you without a big hand – and so you should be inclined to start making re-steals against big stacks who attack you later on, but be hesitant about calling a short stack who goes all-in after you raise.

Bully has all the chips on his shoulder

If you were very loose and aggressive early and it paid off though, then you'll have both the chips and the fearless image to continue bullying people. But you will also need to avoid getting trapped in hands as well as knowing when to call a re-raise, either because you think your hand is better and they're making a re-steal, or you just want to send out the message that you're not leaving chips behind in a pot, and that anyone who raises you might soon be walking out the door.

Of course, behind all these concepts also lie the odds you're getting in any situation and the players you face, and so you need to have a good idea of both how many big blinds each stack has, and where your areas of influence on the table are.

For example, if you have a big stack and the player four to your left does too but those in between don't, you'd be looking to attack from the button and the cut-off seat with a wide range of hands, but be more circumspect after that position. However, if those three players had fewer than ten big blinds you might also be more cautious, as raising could commit you to calling a re-raise all-in with a poor hand.

➤ yourself needing to pass a lot of hands. A-10 under the gun? A 33% chance of being in bad shape to a bigger Ace or pair – so fold it. 7-7 in late position when a solid player has raised early? You're probably no longer getting odds to call to hit a set, so why risk giving valuable chips away when you're either even money or behind and there are few good flops for you?

Fishing for chips

At this point you might also risk becoming dangerously low if things don't go well, and so short-stack play becomes key here, where you usually only have one move left – all in! Remember, though, that 'putting your chips in well' in this type of spot is a key attribute of a top player, and so you need to be keeping an eye on who plays what hands when, what position you're in and what the preceding action means, in order to find the best spot.

> In freezeout tournaments you need to make a stand at some point and you must be prepared to 'go out like a lion, not a lamb'

Crucially, you also need to know how many more rounds you are likely to survive without anteing away, as in freezeout tournaments you need to make a stand at some point and be prepared to 'go out like a lion, not a lamb'. As a rule of thumb then, going below ten big blinds is usually a good time to revert to an all-in strategy, and with less than five you might want to start counting how many more hands you can reasonably wait to get in a pot without making a comeback improbable.

As the money comes into view, things usually start to change again. Which is, of course, because of the payout structure – obviously no one wants to go home empty-handed and so the value of chips and the importance of stack size is exaggerated at

this point, with the well-chipped or fearless players raising more and the timid or short-stacked ones trying to hold on.

Your stack will usually have something to do with how you play at this stage, but you should remember from the outset that this point is likely to arrive eventually, and that it helps if you play for stakes that don't scare you in the first place. For example, in very big events with online satellite qualifiers it's typical to see pros amass large amounts of chips at this stage, at the expense of amateurs for whom surviving to get their $10,000 buy-in back is a result in itself.

One effect of this stage of the game is usually a vast bottlenecking of the field as players dig their heels in, sometimes to ridiculous extents. But if you do try to hang on remember, though, that once you've made the money the payouts often don't rise significantly until the final. Nor should you forget that, especially since the tables will start to play short-handed as fewer remain, this is the time to gamble if you get a reasonable opportunity in the hope of really going for gold!

The final word

So you've made the final table then – great, this is what poker's all about, you might think. This is why you started playing. But remember that all of the money is in the top positions, and that you should therefore keep looking for opportunities to conquer the mountain, rather than just to climb up another rung on the ladder.

Other than that, you will know as a dedicated online player that, excepting the fact that you get paid handsomely wherever you finish, you're now more or less just playing one giant sit&go.   ❖

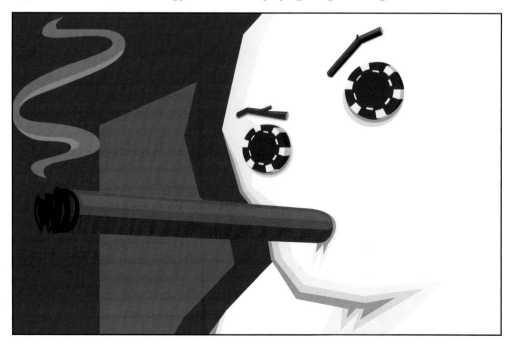

vc poker.com

"No matter what time I log-on, I can always find the game I want without having to wait."

The Tooting Tiger AKA Josh Kennedy, 24 year old sales manager from London.

VC Poker offers such a wide range of games and tournaments that you'll be spoilt for choice no matter what sort of game you're after. And with tens of thousands of people logging on each day, you'll always be able to find plenty of willing opponents.

vcpoker.com

Victor Chandler

DON'T PLAY LIKE A LOSER!

What are the three classic mistakes made by players who are nervous, inexperienced or just plain bad? Poker expert **Andrew NS Glazer** reveals the tell-tale signs of a tournament sucker. If you spot someone else playing like this, go in for the kill. And if *you're* playing like this – stop it!

Thanks in no small part to television, poker tournaments are now more popular than ever. Even many good money players – who used to shun tournaments, fearing that their profitable anonymity might vanish – can no longer ignore them. The massive amounts of prize money on offer, as well as the potential benefits from resultant corporate sponsorship are simply too alluring.

If you're an experienced player, what are some of the most common errors you can expect the huge influx of new players to make, and what can you do about them?

1 NOT UNDERSTANDING WHEN SOMEONE ELSE IS POT-COMMITTED

Ever since a friend mentioned this poker faux pas to me a few months ago, I have been watching carefully for it. Here's a good example, taken from an online tournament I was playing recently.

I held A-J suited on the button, an above-average hand to be sure, but nothing overwhelming either; against good players it's a trouble hand because you're almost sure to be out-kicked if another Ace is in play, you're a small underdog to most pairs, and you're not that big a favourite when you are up against two other non-paired cards. For example, A-J suited isn't even 2/1 against 8-7 off suit, even though it looks so much better.

Because the button so often tries to steal, however, A-J suited looks pretty good – people will play with you with inferior hands. I had $1,900 in front of me, and raised the big blind's $400 up to $1,200. The big blind moved in, I suppose thinking that there was a chance I could let the hand go, but with $2,600 already in the pot, it's far

from easy to get me to throw almost any hand away, I can tell you. The big blind had 2-4 suited.

If I had moved in, would the big blind have played? Calling with small pairs is one of the worst plays in poker, but because there was almost no chance I would fold, this was in essence what he was doing. Nonetheless, because he was a player I didn't know, I shouldn't have assumed he knew the meaning of 'pot-committed' and just moved my whole stack in.

If you have a hand where your raise does commit you to the pot, you might as well go ahead and move all-in with it. If you're winning, you'll win more, and if you're losing, there's a bigger chance that your opponent will fold.

2 UNDERBETTING THE POT

Earlier in this same tournament, I had flat called from the button with that same trouble hand, A-J suited.

The player just to my right, the cut-off seat, had raised it from $30 to $150. I had played with this guy enough times before to guess that this was one of those rare situations where a call was correct instead of a raise or fold. The big blind also played along.

The flop came small and raggy, something like 9, 6, 3. The big blind led out for $30. The cut-off called. There was $525 in the pot. For $30, I was going to look at another card. A deuce came off on the turn, and the big blind again bet $30. The cut-off folded. I just could not imagine what kind of hand could warrant a $30 bet, and so even though I thought there was a decent chance I was getting milked (or set up for a trap), I didn't fold.

A Queen hit the river, and here it came again: $30. I can honestly say that I called 99.98% sure I was beaten. For $30, I wanted to see what the big blind had been doing, in case I faced him again. He turned over K-10, and I was startled when the chips were pushed my way. This had been a pure curiosity call. I was not calling for the size of the pot. I just wanted to know.

I do admit, I considered throwing the hand away, and so the big blind was taking a very inexpensive shot at stealing the pot, but the pot was just too large to try this play. I had plenty of chips. $30 wasn't going to mean a thing. If he had bet just $100, my hand would probably have gone in the muck.

The lesson here? If you're going to try to steal a pot with a garbage hand, you have to make sure that you make

▼ If you've got the nuts, go in hard!

◄ Tense, nervous headache? Next time, don't try to win a hand with garbage using stupidly small bets

I suspect this fellow wasn't even thinking about his Kings as outs; he was, as I've seen with so many players, just too excited about having a big draw. Draws are death in tournaments. They might be fine in your limit money game, where six people see the flop, but calling with a draw is just asking to be eliminated. There's no chance to win with your bet: your hand has to hold up, and you haven't made a hand yet.

Recognising that you're playing someone who will call big bets with draws is a double-edged sword. You may not want to bet if you don't really want the action. If you can make the drawer's price terrible, though, the play is worthwhile. Where you can really find an edge is when you locate someone who will call with a draw with just one card to come, rather than two. Just hope you can get either of these guys on your left, and bet them for value until the cows come home.

> I wouldn't argue too strongly with someone who felt that calling a huge bet with a pure draw, even a draw to the nuts, is actually the worst play in poker

Even if the pot had been large enough to offer my opponent fair pot odds, you're not looking for fair pot odds situations in tournaments either. Chips are just too difficult to replenish, and only a weak player would gamble like that.

It can be tough to let your hand go if you haven't been catching cards or hitting flops. If you bet enough to stand a very good chance of winning with the bet, you can consider it. Calling for most or all of your stack with a draw is only slightly better than calling with small pairs. At least when you call with your draw, if it *is* the nut draw, you don't risk running into a dominated hand situation.

I wouldn't argue too strongly with someone who felt that calling a huge bet with a pure draw, even a draw to the nuts, is actually the worst play in poker. The pot odds you're getting might prove to be a mitigating factor, because even if it's your whole stack you're risking, if four people have already gone all-in and you have the nut-flush draw (knowing you're up against at least one set, possibly more, so suited cards that pair the board are no use to you), the play can be right.

But you're very rarely going to run into that sort of situation. Big-bet poker is usually heads-up, and when you can't replenish your stack, merely calling with a hand that isn't yet a hand usually spells doom.

it expensive enough so that the other player isn't likely to call just for the information he'll gain by doing so.

3 CALLING WITH DRAWS

I see tournament novices make this mistake time and time again.

We're in the same tournament, and this time I manage to get involved with something other than A-J, although not by much: A-Q, in the $50 big blind. Two players had limped, and I decided to look at the flop without a raise, figuring I wouldn't be placed on this particular hand.

The flop came 5♦, 4♠, Q♦; pretty fair, except for the flush draw. The player to my left was fairly aggressive and I figured he would bet my pot for me. I

checked, and sure enough, he bet $100. The other limper called, and I moved in, a raise of about $1,000. I didn't want to give a flush draw the right price to play.

The player on my left called so fast that I assumed he either had the same hand or a small set. The third player got out, and my opponent turned over K♦-9♦: a non-nut-flush draw. There was $550 in the pot, and he was going to have to put $1,000 in to go for the hand.

There was a pretty reasonable case for him to think that he had outs other than diamonds, that is, for him to think that the other three Kings were also outs. This gave him 12 outs and roughly 46% winning chances, although if I had been semi-bluffing with the nut-flush draw, certainly a realistic possibility, he would have been in bad shape.

The duel in poker's crown

Heads-up play, especially in a no-limit game, is the ultimate poker battle, says **Phil Shaw**. Read our in-depth guide to the game and reap the rewards next time you play one-on-one

A ring game of poker can be nerve-jangling enough, but if you really want to get closely acquainted with the edge of your seat, heads-up (one-on-one) poker is the game for you. As in any duel, there can be only one winner, and there's no-one else to hide behind. Passing every hand or playing passively will quickly seal your defeat, and that's why beginners – even those experienced in other forms of poker – rarely have much success. They simply don't adjust to playing against only one person and let their opponent run over them.

Experience counts

If you find yourself up against a passive, inexperienced beginner in a heads-up game, it is a sensible strategy to just raise as often as possible pre-flop and bet on the flop (without making this too obvious). Show them you have a hand whenever possible and back off at the first sign of strength from them. This will rapidly build your stack and erode theirs. Remember that the odds of them starting with a pair are 16/1 against, and that if they have two unpaired cards the chances of flopping a pair are around 2/1 against.

Even if they do start with or make a pair, when the flop comes down, the chances are it will be so small that they will still fold to a bet because of all the overcards! If they have a draw it is also likely that they will play it weakly, and you will simply be able to keep betting, or check and fold to a bet if you think they have made it. In tournament play, after you have used this tactic successfully and gained a big lead you would then be able to take a cheap shot at knocking them out by playing an all-in hand, or if they realise what's happening and become overly aggressive (which happens quite often) you can slow down a bit and prepare to trap them with a big hand.

Between more experienced players, however, the game is played much tighter and tougher. This often results in a war of attrition, with neither player getting too far out of line or being prepared to surrender a hand too easily. In this situation, you want to play solid, aggressive poker and steal as many pots as possible. It is also best to bear in mind that early on, very big pots will usually mean very big hands, so it's important not to over commit and let yourself get on the wrong end of a decisive confrontation.

It's usually very hard to lay down a smaller full house to a bigger one, or even a flush or straight on a paired board as the chances of such a clash of hands is tiny, but you must always bear in mind that your opponent could

be trapping you with a hand of this sort, or could have started out with Aces or Kings in a hand where it's suddenly hard to see how the community cards have helped them.

This is heads-up in a nutshell, and it distils the two essential aims of poker into a pure form: disguising your own hand, and figuring out your opponent's.

Poker at its purest

In heads-up play, then, the fact that poker is all about situation and psychology is most apparent, and your constant aim is to simultaneously confuse your opponent and understand his actions. If you are a novice player, it's probably best to get some experience of this playing in ring games or normal tournaments first, but if you already play a good general game, it's easily possible to do this.

First of all, you must recognise that in most heads-up matches, the same player is both the button and the small blind. That puts the button player at a major advantage, since whoever holds the button gets to act first before the flop, where they can steal the blinds or raise first. They then get the benefit of seeing what their opponent does first on the flop.

This is almost as powerful as having the serve in tennis and you should use it to your advantage whenever

possible, by raising pre-flop and creating bigger pots with most playable hands – any Ace, face cards like Q-J, K-J, or even Q-10 and K-9 are all raise-worthy, while raising with drawing hands like 8♥-9♥ or T♣-7♣ will add an extra dimension to your game by making you harder to read. Only unplayable garbage like 8-2 off-suit should be folded, because against just one opponent, the average starting hand they will have is so low.

It's quite acceptable in heads-up to call with a single face card or something you wouldn't dream of playing in a ring game, just to see how the hand develops – although, you wouldn't normally want to call big raises or play big pots with such a hand unless it turns into a monster. Then, if the flop connects with your hand in any way and your opponent checks, you can simply bet it (you should also bet some of the time with no hand, as there is a good chance the other player has missed and is checking out of weakness).

You may find yourself betting a good hand, a weak hand, a draw or nothing at all, but what is important is that by

> **Heads-up is often a war of attrition, with neither player getting out of line or being prepared to surrender a hand too easily**

doing so, you force your opponent to make a tough decision. If they call and you sense weakness, it is normally right to bet again – some players will call on the flop just to see if you show weakness on the turn, so you must leave no doubt in their mind. If they are drawing, a bet on the turn, around the size of the pot, will usually make it incorrect for them to continue, providing the turn card looks unlikely to have helped them. If you are check-raised or bet into at any point, you must base your decision on what you know about your opponent, whether your hand justifies playing on, or whether moving all-in would force them to fold.

Folding a few times in these spots is no big deal, as you will succeed in stealing other pots to stay ahead in chips. What matters is that you are creating a situation where your opponent feels forced to play back at you out of position. Then, at some point, you will have a big hand to trap them with. For this reason, it is often a good idea to bet a very strong hand as well, perhaps making a small bet (known as a 'weak lead'). This may incite your opponent to raise what he thinks is an attempt to buy the pot cheaply, or even making a very big bet that looks like an outright bluff. You should try to make the move as ➤

➤ indistinguishable as possible from how you have acted in the last few hands that you've played.

Your chances of success with this move will improve if you have shown a few bluffs recently. It also helps if you have convinced your opponent that you are an aggressive maniac or have no idea what you are doing!

Off the button

By contrast, out of position, you need to act more defensively to avoid your opponent's traps, and try to trap him with strong hands when he overplays his position. Hands you would raise with from the button pre-flop should be played slower (unless they are very strong). You should also try to keep the pots smaller by checking more often when you have a weak hand or a draw, and usually only check-raising with very strong holdings. If your opponent is raising frequently from the button, you will need to call a few times with slightly weaker hands than you would like in order to send the message that you cannot be run over. Don't, however, go too far afterwards unless you make something.

In short, you must turn your opponent's desire to attack against them by playing the defensive role and checking more often in most situations before either folding, calling or raising. If you call a raise initially, then miss and fold to a bet, you have just taken a cheap flop, since you already had money invested in the big blind. If you call and sense weakness, you can bet first at either the turn or river and try to take the pot, or if you are very strong you can check-raise. If you have a reasonably strong (but not great) hand, you could also call all the way. This will let your opponent bluff off their money to you at minimal risk, as long as you think you are still ahead and the risk of a draw succeeding is minimal.

The key to heads-up is using situation and psychology to your advantage. The cards matter less than in any other type of play

Of course, playing this general style will make your opponent realise you are taking a defensive role, so you don't necessarily need a hand to stay involved. You can call a bet on the flop with the intent of bluffing first later (especially on the river if your opponent checks the turn, as this may indicate they thought you were going for a check-raise on the turn), or check-raise with nothing if you are confident it will cause a bluff to fold. This last move (known as the 're-bluff') is a high risk venture, but all top players use it at some point and it is particularly suited to this heads-up situation. That's because your opponent actually expects you to try to trap at some point, and will be wary enough to let a few hands go!

Going for the kill

A heads-up tournament will soon reach a situation where one player has a significant chip lead and is preparing to move in to polish his opponent off. A useful rule of thumb here is that going below a 3/1 chip deficit is highly dangerous, as even if you double up at some point, you will still be behind. In this position, you will really need to draw a line in the sand as soon as you possibly can and refuse to be eroded any more, usually by trying to force a favourable all-in hand. The big stack will be trying to trap you by slow playing or using the button effectively, but from his position of power he is less likely to gamble in a marginal situation. You can use this to your advantage to build back up by moving all-in more frequently, especially if the blinds have got quite big.

The correct strategy if you are the big stack here is to continue applying pressure wherever possible with bets in situations where you can either steal small pots or fold to a raise without giving too many chips up. You want to either erode the short stack to the point where a double through will still leave a massive chip deficit and you can take a cheap shot at them, or force them into making a final mistake against a strong hand.

The key to heads-up is remembering to use both situation and psychology to your advantage. The cards matter less than in any other type of play, and the roles of the two players are more strongly defined, either by position or by chips. Bear this in mind and play fearless, solid poker and you will not only succeed in heads-up play most of the time, but you will also sharpen your general game immeasurably. It's a win-win situation. ❄

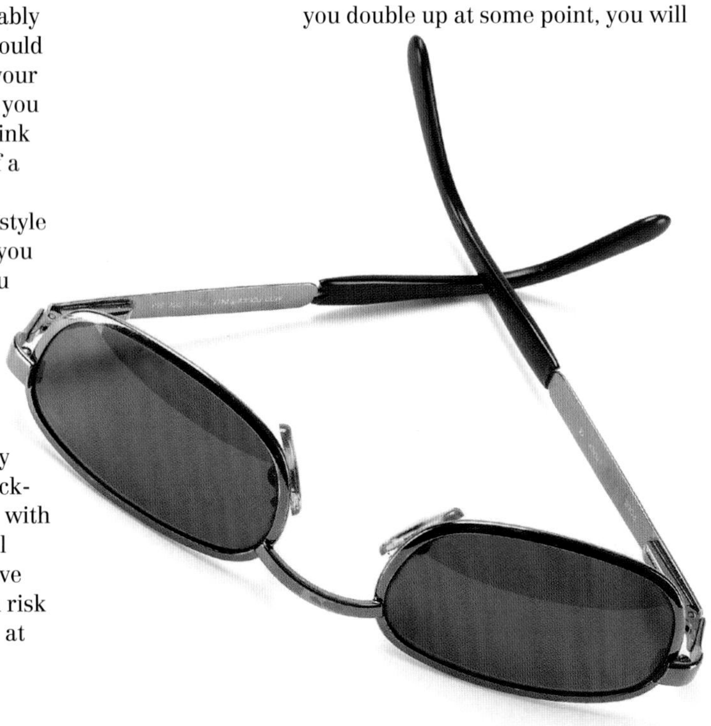

KNOW THE HEADS-UP HANDS

You will have seen these odds before but you can't know them well enough in heads-up play

In tournament poker, one area that all top players know inside out is the odds of their hand winning in all-in situations against other hands. Most of them don't like playing all-ins that are close to even money and some will even fold as a decent favourite rather than risk a big all-in early on. For most players, even the greats, though, there comes a point in a tournament when playing an all-in is necessary, and needless to say you should always be looking to be a clear favourite when this happens! Below is a list of possible confrontations and the odds, so that you don't find yourself on the wrong end of a losing proposition. Odds on the turn are omitted, as these can simply be calculated as the number of outs for and against you out of the remaining 44 cards in the deck.

PRE-FLOP

Hands	Win	Lose	Draw
A♣-A♦ vs K♣-K♠	81.5	18	0.5
A♣-A♦ vs Q♠-J♠	80	19.5	0.5
A♥-A♦ vs K♣-T♥	86	13.5	0.5
A♣-K♣ vs A♠-7♥	72.5	23	4.5
A♠-6♦ vs A♠-2♣	38	28	34
A♣-K♣ vs 2♥-2♣	50	49.5	0.5
A♣-K♠ vs Q♠-Q♣	43.5	56	0.5
A♥-K♣ vs 8♥-9♥	61	38.5	0.5
A♣-J♥ vs Q♠-9♠	58.5	41	0.5
A♣-6♠ vs 9♥-T♥	51.5	48	0.5

ON THE FLOP

Hand	Flop	Win	Lose	Draw
A♥-A♣ vs 9♣-9♦	7♠, 3♦, 2♥	91.5	8.5	
A♥-A♣ vs 9♣-9♦	9♠, 3♦, 2♥	10	90	
A♥-A♠ vs 7♣-8♣	9♣, 6♣, 2♠	56.5	43.5	
A♥-K♥ vs 9♠-9♦	7♥, 3♦, 2♥	45	55	
A♥-3♥ vs 9♠-9♦	7♥, 3♦, 2♥	47.5	52.5	
A♠-J♣ vs K♠-J♥	J♦, 4♠, 3♥	86.5	12	1.5
A♥-A♣ vs 9♠-7♠	6♥, 8♣, 2♦	66	34	
A♥-A♣ vs 9♠-7♠	9♣, 8♠, 6♠	33.5	64.5	2
A♥-A♣ vs 9♠-7♠	K♠, 2♠, 4♦	63.5	36.5	
9♠-9♥ vs A♣-3♠	A♥, 7♠, 4♦	9	91	

Pull up your blinds

How do you avoid throwing away money on the big and small blinds at the start of a hand? Poker expert **Andrew NS Glazer** emerges from a smoky room to reveal all

Blinds in hold'em serve a purpose similar to antes in stud games: they create an incentive for a player to invest and/or attack. Without any 'starter money', there would be little incentive for an intelligent player to make the first bet, even with a very good hand. If everyone else folds, he's won nothing. Without blinds or antes, the first bet is merely a target, and the other players could safely fold without an unbeatable hand.

By forcing the player to the dealer's left to post a small blind (SB) and the player to *his* left to pay a big blind (BB – usually double the small blind), hold'em becomes much more interesting and action-filled. Each hand begins as a battle for the blinds, and once that battle begins, the pot starts growing, and the reasons to play grow with it.

Low-stakes games rarely end with the first raise; in high-stakes games, especially no-limit tournament final tables, the first raise often does end the hand.

> **If you had to post a big blind on every hand, you'd get slaughtered. You're in early position and investing chips before you see your cards**

Even though blinds serve a purpose similar to antes, they function quite differently. Antes are 'dead money.' Anteing merely entitles you to receive cards; you still must make a bet to engage in the action. If you post one of the blinds, however, your money counts as a bet (it's 'live'). If you post the BB, and no one else plays, you then win the hand. You won't have won much – only the SB (which is usually half the size of the BB, although it can vary from one-third to two-thirds of its size). While any win helps, of course, more often the fact that your blind money counts as a bet will make getting involved in many other hands easier, because you're getting to play for a discount price.

Correct blind play: making the best of a bad situation

When, why, and how you should play when you're getting that discount is a widely misunderstood subject. Let's start with a key principle behind correct blind play. Some situations are natural money losers, and the hands when you post the blinds fall into that category. If you had to post the BB on every hand, you'd get slaughtered: you're in early position (bad), and investing money before you see your cards (also bad). Over the long haul, you *will* lose money on your blind hands – not every time, of course, but on balance. The key is to lose as little as possible, so you can make money overall by taking advantage of your premium situations, like when you sit in late position.

Let's start with an elementary blind-play decision. You've posted the $30 BB in a no-limit hold'em game; your neighbour to the right has posted the $15 SB. Everyone folds around to the button, who decides to raise it to a total of $90 (a $60 raise). The small blind folds, and now it's up to you. Does this hand continue, or does the button win $45?

Understand the risks

Assuming that you have a plausible hand (more on that in a moment), you have to then assess your risk/reward ratio, and to do that, you have to decide whether you're going to try to win the pot by calling and then winning on the flop, or by raising and trying to win right away.

Raising will cost you $60 plus the amount you raise; let's say you raise an additional $180, a total bet of $240. The tricky part is to understand what

▲ Learning how to play the big and small blinds is something that poor poker players often don't bother doing. Don't make the same mistake

you're trying to win with your raise: you're trying to claim only $135. Some people mistakenly think 'After I call, my raise is giving me a shot at a $195 pot' (in other words, thinking that their $180 raise might buy them $195). They're wrong: the pot only becomes $195 after you call. Your $240 bet is a shot at the money already in the pot, and that was only $135 when you made your move!

There's a mighty big difference between risking $180 to win $195 and risking $240 to win $135. The first play (were the numbers accurate) doesn't even have to succeed half the ➤

easy or hard it is to outplay your opponents on the flop. How well you think you can get 'paid off' when you hit your hand also makes a huge difference, and remember, it's much harder to get paid off handsomely when you're acting out of position – and that's exactly what you're doing when playing from the blind.

Defending blinds ain't easy – no matter what the game

In limit poker, it initially seems easier to defend the blinds because the investment odds are usually better. The button can't raise as much, so you don't face as much immediate pressure. The problems in analysing limit poker defending don't end there, though. It's much harder to win the pot with a re-raise, because the amount you're re-raising isn't enough to knock out someone who had raised from the button; even if he was stealing, he'll usually call and look at the flop.

Similarly, when you get a favourable flop, you can't usually win it with one bet. You will have to risk seeing a turn card also, and make a second bet. In limit poker, the raiser can't put as much pressure on you, but you can't put as much pressure on him. You'll probably have to attack him twice, and be out of position each time.

That's why even though the relative cheapness makes it first appear easier to defend the blinds in limit poker, before the hand is over, it winds up being probably just as hard as in no limit or pot limit. You just face a different collection of problems. Playing the hand out of position on the flop, turn, and (if you get that far) the river is a huge disadvantage. Each time the opportunity comes to bet, you are going to have to act first. Your opponent will have more information than you when it's his turn to act, and that's very bad news.

Position is all-important

Suppose you call and you do hit the flop. Do you bet? If you do, your opponent still has most of the power and options. If his hand missed the flop, he might concede, and you'll only win the money that was in the pot to start. If he hit the flop too he can raise, and now where are you? Do you call a re-raise? The problem will become even more troublesome on the turn. You bet the flop, but your opponent didn't go away. Assuming the turn card doesn't help you, where do you go? Do you bet again, hoping to scare your opponent off? Do you show weakness by checking? To win the

➤ time to be profitable. The second has to work 64% of the time just to break even (actually a bit more than that when you remember you're paying a rake).

The maths changes when you try to win by calling and then making a decision on the flop. Your $60 call cannot win the pot. All calling does is give you the right to make a play later in the hand, and that will necessarily mean risking more money then. If the flop is favourable enough, it might not be much of a risk; if the flop is unfavourable, your money may be gone

and your only remaining chance will be an opportunity to lose more.

Your $60 call creates a $195 pot. If you assume that you will only make a move at the pot when the flop is favourable (good players' actions are more complex than that), you can call, in a purely mathematical sense, if the flop will be favourable 30.8% of the time (60 divided by 195). Whether hitting a flop is easier or more difficult than that depends to some extent on your hand, and to some extent on how

THE GOLDEN RULES FOR PLAYING FROM THE BLINDS

- Most players defend their blinds too often, but you must defend often enough to ward off automatic attacks.
- It's marginally easier to defend your blind in a limit game or in a multi-way pot, because you are receiving much better pot odds, but that still doesn't make playing the blinds a winning position.
- Most players fail to recognize the huge inherent weaknesses involved when playing the remainder of the hand out of

position; a decision to defend involves consideration of what will happen on future betting rounds.
- Defending doesn't just mean calling; attack is often the best form of defence. Often, it is correct to 'defend' with a raise.
- When selecting hands with which to defend, be wary of hands that are likely to be dominated, like Aces or Kings with bad kickers. Look more favourably on connected middle cards or small pairs.

hand playing out of position is far harder than most people realise. Worse still, when you do win, you usually win much less than you could have won if you had been the final player to act, rather than the first.

Because of the position problem, most players defend their blinds far too often. They see that they already have some money invested, and are getting a 'discount' on their call, but fail to think the hand all the way through. They may be getting a discount, but they are getting a discount on damaged goods. Efforts to show that you can't be 'pushed around' in the blind can be very costly. Most players would win much more (or lose much less) if they defended their blinds less.

Because good poker advice is rarely black and white, you shouldn't turn into an easy target every time you hold the blind. If you don't defend at least occasionally, you can be certain that you will be attacked every time, and that will cost you more money. The occasional call, or better still the occasional re-raise, will alert the late-position players that your blind is not free for the taking.

Picking your spots

Given that you must defend sometimes, what sort of hands should you defend with? I wish I could give you a simple guideline like, 'You should defend your blind 31% of the time,' but no such rule exists, because how much defending you need to do is a factor of how much attacking the other players choose to do.

Some defendable hands are obvious, however. If you get dealt a big pair or A-K or A-Q suited, your hand

practically plays itself. If you won't re-raise with those hands, you're too timid to play winning poker.

Unfortunately, you won't be dealt these strong hands as often as you need to defend your blind, so you'll need to select some other hands to defend with. Choosing the right hands is very important, and many players instinctively make the wrong choice.

> **Most players defend their blinds far too often. Sure, they get a 'discount' on their call, but that's a discount on damaged goods**

Even though A-4 is a better heads-up hand than J-10, you're much better off defending with the J-10. Why? On many occasions when a late-position player attacks, if he has an Ace, it's a big Ace. That means that if you get the 'apparently' good flop of A, 9, 5, you might wind up losing a fortune to someone who was raising with A-K. Even though Aces and Kings look like excellent 'defending' cards, unless you have a strong kicker, you run too much risk of finding yourself in a 'dominated hand' position.

A hand like J-10 is less likely to contain the same key cards as your attacker's. If an Ace hits the flop, you can get away from your hand. If the flop comes 10, 4, 2, the player who raised you with A-Q has nothing – and it's far more likely that a late-position raise will come from someone holding two big cards than from someone holding a big pair.

As a result, 'unpredictable' but potentially

useful hands like J-10 or even 5-6 are probably better defending hands than something like A-2 or K-3. If you play A-2 and an Ace flops, you'll only get action when your hand is in big trouble. If you play something 'tricky' like 7-8, you might wind up crushing someone who raised from late position with A-K when the flop comes A, 7, 8. You can also win pots from A-K raisers who are afraid to slow down when the flop comes 8, 3, 2. You'll pay dearly if the raiser held K-K, but again remember that late-position raises are more likely to come from players holding two big cards than from a big pair. Naturally, if the raiser held K-K and the flop comes 8, 8, 3, your call with 7-8 puts you in position to win a fortune from players who don't expect you to be holding an eight.

How many are queuing up to hit you?

The next important point to consider when defending your blind is in a sense a variation on the pot-odds question: how many people have attacked so far? If in a limit game a mid-position player raises to $60, and three players flat-call that raise, the first thing you should do is realise you've found a good game, because flat-calling two bets is usually a weak play. If your hand is strong enough to call two bets, it is likely that it is strong enough to take the initiative to make it three bets.

Let's leave the juicy game issue aside, though, and realise that the multi-player situation changes your pot odds considerably. With four players in for $60 and a folded $15 small blind, the pot contains $285 when you ponder putting in the extra $30. These pot odds are so wonderful that you can call with almost any kind of reasonable hand; I'd even call with something as woeful as 3-2 (but not 7-2; against multi-player fields, you want hands that can make straights or flushes).

Most of the time, your weak hand will be worthless on the flop, but when you do hit it, the rich pot tends to get richer: players will stay in with you, chasing for the size of the pot, and instead of $285, you'll probably win $500 or $600 in a limit game. In a pot-limit or no-limit game, your speculative holding can easily bust someone who makes the mistake of forgetting that hold'em is not a two-card game, but a seven-card game. ❁

GET THE DROP ON THE FLOPS

The key to winning poker games often lies in how you play after the flop, but how do you know which hands are worth playing? **Phil Shaw** takes you through the basics

Everyone knows poker is a game that takes a minute to learn and a lifetime to master. The main reason for this dichotomy is the fact that you start out with only two cards, but then have to estimate their value combined with the flop, turn and river, where the possibilities are myriad and keep altering (see Hand combinations box, right).

That's why playing after the flop is the key to real poker prowess and profit. So a successful player has to be confident in his reads – and know when he's putting himself in too much danger. This type of skill doesn't come easily, so a good place to start is to get a feel for the possibilities that lie in a given hand of poker. After all, you need to be able to see the whole of a map to understand where you're situated on it. To this end, we're going to run through the rankings

of poker hands, but with some guidance on how strong you can expect each hand to be in certain situations.

Ace high

This isn't much of a hand; indeed, it's no hand at all in a multi-way pot. Remember that it may still be a winning hand at the river in a heads-up pot if there's little action after the flop – and be prepared to pick off a likely bluff. Nevertheless, don't take much heat with this one.

Top pair

Depending on the quality of the pair and kicker, as well as the texture of the board, a top-pair hand is often a winner on the flop but is often behind by the time the river comes. Bet strongly early on to find out where you stand, but be prepared to release if your hand is weak and someone plays you back on a flop with few draws, or if many players are still in and the betting heats up. If you have A-K on a flop, such as A-10-2 off-suit, though, your hand is very strong, so be prepared to go all-in with it if the blinds are high in a tournament. In a deep-stacked cash game or tournament, beware of experienced players, as this is a classic way of losing all your chips, usually to a set or two pair.

Two pair

Flopping two pair when you didn't start with one in the hole makes for a very strong and deceptive holding, but you can still be in danger by the river because of straight, flush and better two-pair possibilities. Also, if the board pairs with a card you don't have, a low two-pair can be ruined. Try to balance getting the most for the hand with turning the heat up before the board gets too dangerous.

Trips

Flopping trips from a pair in the hole is a deceptive, powerhouse hand, and one that's rarely beaten on the flop. However, as with two pair, you need to get the most for it as quickly as possible, as straight and flush possibilities can still ruin it. Trips over trips is rare, but is a realistic worry in a deep cash game. Making trips from a pair on the board is also a strong hand (although bear in mind your kicker if the action gets big), but, as it's so obvious, it's harder to profit from, so you should just try to milk whatever you can.

Straight

A well-disguised straight can be a goldmine (for example, you have 9-7 and the board comes 8, J, 6, 5), but it suffers from being vulnerable to flushes and full houses. The best plan is to make the most of it before the board pairs or flushes, or be prepared to play it more modestly and lose a little value. Obvious straights – let's say you have A-10 and the board comes 6, 7, 8, 9 – are of little value unless you're an aggressive bluffing player who can make it look like you're just trying to buy the pot.

Flush

A strong hand, but one that lacks disguise unless the flush comes backdoor. Let's say you have A♠-7♠ and the board comes 10♠, 8♣, 4♥, J♠, 2♠, and again benefits aggressive players who may just be bluffing. Four flushes on the board are likely to have hit someone, and so are similar to four straights, but the rank of the suited card will determine who wins. If you don't have the Ace, play it passively and be prepared to check and call on the river in situations where you have a good chance of being ahead.

> ## A well-disguised straight can be a goldmine (you have 9-7 and the board comes 8, J, 6, 5, say), but it's vulnerable to flushes and full houses

Full house

A virtually impregnable hand, and ideal for slow play, as higher hands are unlikely, and you need to let more cards come for your opponents to make a good second-best hand. The only time you need to be cautious is when the stacks are very deep and bigger houses are possible: judge it wrong and you could have an early night.

Quads

Virtually unbeatable. Tales of quads losing to bigger quads or a straight flush are as likely as an A-lister doing a reality TV show. Sadly, it's often also difficult to get paid with quads, as you have the board strangled. So give your opponents as many opportunities as possible to make a hand and try to squeeze them for whatever you can get.

Straight flush

Unless you've somehow managed to walk into a scene from *Lock, Stock and Two Smoking Barrels*, you'll be laughing all the way to the bank with a straight flush. The only problem will be finding a mug to call you down!

HAND COMBINATIONS
WHAT ARE THE ODDS?

At its most basic level, poker is a numbers game. Here are some stats illustrating the expanding possibilities throughout a hand

Being dealt the same hole cards several times in a night isn't unusual, but the combinations made possible by the river mean you could play for a lifetime and still not see exactly the same thing happen twice in a full hand.

Possibilities

● **Hole card combinations**
(if you overlook the suits of the cards you're dealt) **169**

● **Hole card combinations**
(if you account for the suits of the cards you're dealt) **1,326**

● **Starting hands for your opponents**
(if you account for the suits of the cards you're dealt) **1,225**

● **Flops to your hole cards**
For example, you have A♣-A♣ and the flop comes, say, A♥, 6♦, 6♣ **19,600**

● **Full board combinations**
That is, if you dealt out five cards from the deck – A♥, K♠, 3♦, 6♥, 6♣, say, excluding the two you have in the hole **2,118,760**

● **Five-card hands**
For instance, if you dealt out five cards **2,598,960**

● **Seven-card combinations**
(hole cards plus board)
If you dealt out seven cards **133,784,560**

The fork in the road

Tournament and cash poker games have opposite risks and rewards and understanding the differences is crucial. Premier poker writer **Nolan Dalla** takes you on a journey of discovery

About ten years ago, I drove along the California interstate and came upon a split in the road. Off to my left was the highway leading back to the Pacific Ocean and the San Francisco Bay area – the site of a half-dozen bustling poker rooms filled with live poker action. Off to my right was the highway leading towards the Sierra Nevada Mountains and Reno, the host city of what was, at the time, one of the biggest poker tournaments in the world. I intended to play poker over a long holiday weekend and didn't know which direction to go.

Left or right? San Francisco or Reno? Cash games or tournaments?

The proverbial 'fork in the road' is a dilemma for many poker players the world over. Cash games and tournaments are both appealing in their own right. They also include an entirely opposite set of risks and potential rewards. For instance, the short-term financial risks are usually

less in tournaments, since players can only lose up to a certain amount of money (the buy-in).

However, the long-term financial risks are actually much greater in tournaments, since it is much more difficult to maintain a consistent level of performance which will ensure a profit. In short, poker tournaments involve greater financial swings (also known as 'variance') for players than any cash game.

The rewards of poker tournaments and cash games are also quite the contrary. Poker tournaments usually offer more prize money to winners and the top finishers, and certainly more public exposure than cash games. In the biggest poker tournaments with the highest buy-ins, the winner's life can literally change within a single day. A certain (former)

> **Fame and fortune follows tournament champions while cash players often wallow in anonymity**

accountant named Chris Moneymaker and a certain (former) corporate attorney named Greg Raymer went from working regular nine to five jobs to instant millionaires because of their victories in a poker tournament.

So fame and fortune follows tournament champions, while cash-game players often wallow in anonymity. But there's a downside, too. It's important to remember that for every poker millionaire on television there are thousands of poker wannabes who lack the knowledge and skill to be successful.

The question is – which direction is right for you? Is it better to spend most of your time playing in cash games? Or, is it preferable to enter more poker tournaments and take a shot at the big money? The answer will depend on your poker goals and personal ambitions. In order to make a wise decision, you need to know more about the similarities and differences of poker tournaments and cash games.

A FEW THOUGHTS ABOUT ONLINE POKER

Internet poker is virtually a different poker game from the brick and mortar variety. Internet poker games are:

★ **Faster** Often, twice as many hands are dealt per hour. However, many tournaments employ a set number of hands per round. This is different from live tournaments, which almost always use a time clock.

★ **Wilder** Online players tend to play more loosely than in live-action games. It's much easier to call a bet or raise with the click of a mouse than to physically reach for one's chips and place them into the pot. This dynamic, unique to online poker, creates more bad beats and seemingly inexplicable behaviour than in regular cardrooms.

★ **Based more on relative strength of hands and position rather than tells** Most of the time when playing over the internet, you are up against people you don't know. The screen name across the table may indicate some characteristics about the player – but you never really know who you are playing against. In live action games, strategic decisions are often made based solely on the opponent's appearance and behaviour, otherwise known as tells. These clues do not exist online.

★ **Offers greater variety or choices** The biggest online poker rooms, including *vcpoker.com*, often have hundreds of games going on around the clock. While your local casino may have a dozen or so games going, there are literally thousands of poker games taking place every hour of the day and night on internet poker sites.

This means you have a much easier time changing tables and trying to find the right game. Furthermore, most of the major poker sites offer numerous daily tournaments – including freerolls. While the local casino may have a nightly tournament, a popular site such as *vcpoker.com* may offer hundreds or more tournaments every single day. So you can play poker exactly when it suits you.

The similarities

A rose is a rose is a rose – and poker is poker. Whether it's a cash game or a tournament, a flush still beats a straight and good players beat bad players – in the long run, at least. Winners in both cash games and tournaments have several qualities in common. These include:

● **Practising sound bankroll management** Winning poker players play in the right size game to fit their bankroll. They don't play over their heads in big cash games or take reckless chances by investing too much money in poker tournaments, even though the potential for a big payoff might be tempting.

● **Establishing a tight-aggressive playing style** More often than not, tight-aggressive play wins the money. Tight-aggressive is defined as playing fewer hands than your opponents, but when you do play a hand to (usually) bet and raise aggressively.

This strategy works best, whether you're playing in a cash game or in a poker tournament.

● **Avoid playing marginal hands** The very worst hand to hold in any pot is the second-best hand. This is because the runner-up will invest more and lose more than any player at the table. Therefore, it is crucial to avoid hands that have 'second best' potential – such as Aces with weak kickers (A-2, A-3, and so forth) and marginal face cards (K-J, K-10, and so forth). Being able to avoid trap hands is even more critical in tournaments, since you only have a limited number of chips.

● **Doing the unexpected** Most winning poker players think 'outside the box.' They occasionally make unexpected moves. Playing in a straightforward manner can be profitable in some situations, but beating cash games (especially middle and high-limit games) and winning poker tournaments requires mixing up play and avoiding a predictable strategy. ➤

> The differences

While poker basics may be much the same whatever the circumstances, cash games and tournaments have a number of fundamental differences which must be considered when deciding which venture is preferable. These include:

● **Table and seat selection** Finding the right game is at least half the battle. Beating cash games often requires that you play against opponents who are less skilful. In cash games, you have the luxury of picking favourable games and seats. Furthermore, you can always request a transfer or a seat change if you are in a bad spot. But in tournaments, all seats are assigned and you have no control over your opponents.

● **Time commitments** A poker tournament often requires a full day or evening to complete. This means you must be prepared to sit and play poker for many hours at a time. In cash games, you can quit at any time, whether you are up or down. But poker tournaments endure to the finish, which usually involves a greater commitment of time.

● **Varying strategies at different stages** Cash games essentially require a consistent playing strategy, albeit with some degree of unpredictability. However, there are very different strategies depending on the stage of the tournament (early, middle, and late) and whether or not re-buys are permitted. Optimal strategy can change depending upon factors such as stack sizes, amount of time left in the round, and so forth.

● **Different goals** Assuming you play poker to win and not merely as a recreational pastime, it's important to know players have an extraordinarily diverse array of goals which motivate their decisions at the table. Most cash game goals involve an hourly or session expectation. However, tournament players are often motivated by things other than money – including peer recognition, satisfying competitive instincts, and fame (especially if the tournament is televised or includes an audience). There's nothing wrong with playing poker for reasons other than money – it's just important that we understand all players are not motivated by winning money.

Making the leap from tournaments to cash games

The growing popularity of poker on television has introduced thousands of new players to the nuances of tournament poker. Accordingly, many new players enter tournaments before they've played a single hand of live-action poker. This was unheard of, until a few years ago.

Most poker players of previous generations learned to play poker in cash games first – either at home or at a local casino – before venturing into tournament poker. Now, an entirely new breed of player called the 'tournament specialist' has entered the lexicon of poker lingo.

> A new breed of player called the 'tournament specialist' has entered the lexicon of poker lingo

Making the transition from tournaments to cash games is analogous to shifting the gears of a high-performance sports car down to a family saloon. Like the flashy automobile, tournaments are sexier and more exciting. By contrast, most cash games are more methodical.

For many years, there was a small, but widely-known group of very successful tournament players who were big contributors in cash games. Whatever they won – and sometimes it was six figures or more – was dumped in the cash games. The tournament pros essentially created a cottage industry in poker. The question is – why? How was it possible that a world-class tournament player could be a loser in cash games?

The answer is quite simple. Many players, even the best tournament players to this day, fail to adjust their strategy and style to suit live-action games. They falsely believe they can intimidate opponents and run over the games with the same tactics that are used so effectively in tournaments. But it doesn't work that way.

Making the leap from cash games to tournaments

Hurdling from cash games to tournaments is the conventional stepladder for most poker players. They usually begin playing poker in small cash games and steadily proceed up to the tournament level. Frankly, I believe this approach has certain advantages. Firstly, it allows players to progressively develop their skills and move up gradually to where there is more money as well as added pressure. Most players who are thrust into poker tournaments without developing basic skills, perhaps unsurprisingly, do not fare very well.

The transition from playing cash games to tournaments also requires changes in one's preparation and level of commitment. Since a standard poker tournament may take 12 hours or more to complete, stamina is more important to the tournament player. Cash-game players can take breaks or depart as they wish. But tournament players are potentially faced with a much more demanding ritual that requires extraordinary mental focus. ❖

THE BEST OF BOTH WORLDS

When it comes to choosing what's right for you, flexibility is your friend

This article began with my 'fork in the road' decision as to whether I would to go down the tournament or cash route. In the end, I headed to Reno's big poker tournament. However, when I arrived – the unexpected happened.

Prior to the start of the event that I had planned to enter, I took a seat in a pot-limit cash game. I started to win and continued to win. By the time the tournament started, I had reassessed my situation and decided to stay in the cash game. To cut a long story short, I departed

Reno a few days later with a nice profit, almost all of it coming from that cash game. In fact, I didn't play in a single tournament the whole time I was there.

This illustrates perhaps the most important component of winning poker – which is to always be flexible. You never know what will happen when you arrive at the poker table. Every poker room is in a constant state of flux. Consistently re-evaluating your priorities and responding to the conditions around you is the best poker advice of all.

Staying afloat

The first rule of being a successful poker player is picking the right games in order to keep your bankroll healthy. **Phil Shaw** guides you through the basics

The issue most overlooked by beginner poker players – and a few more experienced ones – is that of bankroll management and game selection. Frequently, though, this is the difference between winning and losing, and between being in action and watching from the rail.

In basic terms a bankroll is a sum of money set aside to play poker, out of which should be enough for you to survive the ups and downs of the game – as well as cover all expenses, tips, and rake or table charges – and allow you to turn a consistent profit. The question of bankroll management and game selection is intimately linked, since the whole concept of a bankroll assumes that you are a winning player overall, and that you can find games that you're both able to beat and almost never likely to go broke in.

If this isn't the case then, from a financial point of view, you would probably do better to find the smallest limits tolerable to you and consider the money you lose (or spend on flights, hotels and so on) as entertainment or education.

Game selection covers a wide selection of issues, and is just as important as how you play during any given hand or session. It may mean playing at the right stakes, the right betting structure or the right type of poker, but most frequently it means playing with the right people (ie those who have money and are a lot worse at poker than you).

The masters of this aspect of poker tend to be those players with the maximum flexibility, who will go just about anywhere for a game and who will play any particular mixture of games in order to keep the weaker players happy. One highly respected UK player recently described another as: 'a master of game selection. He will travel anywhere.'

Which puts him in good company, since this sentiment actually echoes down throughout poker history, right back to the days of the Texas road gamblers. They would happily drive a couple of days straight on hearing of a 'good game', typically living nomadic lives built around travelling wherever the action was.

Nowadays, though, an explosion of popularity and interest in the game has transformed the poker scene, and there's suddenly more action available than ever before. This comes in the form of poker festivals all over the place (meaning many players still live on the road for a big part of the year) and on the internet, where there are already more than 200 sites to choose from and an almost limitless selection of games.

> **The net offers low-expense play, maximum choice, and the option of winning seats in major festival events for a small investment**

‣ Don't get jolly rogered

These two options are very popular with both the professional and recreational players, and tend to both interlink and contrast in their viability.

For example, the internet offers fast, convenient, low-expense play and maximum choice to all, but also the option of winning seats in major festival events for a small investment and an upper limit on stakes. The live festival circuit, in contrast, typically has the biggest tournaments and cash action in one place and the offers the chance to see the world while making a living, but also the most risk of going broke or finding out that your ability – or bankroll – isn't large enough to make it a viable option.

Similarly, while professional players have traditionally always played live, there is now an increasing shift towards the internet game, where they can minimise bankroll fluctuations and multi-table in smaller games so that their 'wages' are more consistent. In this way what could have been a bad week or month live becomes, at worst, a bad couple of days online. Coming at it from the other direction, though, are the internet kids who have built sizeable bankrolls and experience online in short amounts of time and are beginning to hit the live circuit in droves in search of the big action.

The modern poker player therefore finds him or herself in a luxurious situation compared to the road gamblers of yesterday or even the pre-poker-boom pros. New possibilities in game selection and the pressure it takes off your bankroll is a major part of this. Not only are there all-important swathes of new players bringing fresh money into the game, but, for the experienced player, they are accessible from the comfort of your own home and sofa – while they are relaxing or learning the ropes, or against the backdrop of any number of high-adrenalin cities where they flock to in the hope of TV stardom, a 'poker holiday' or, in most cases, simply of hitting the big-time.

WHAT GAMES SHOULD I PLAY?
CASH GAMES

Most professional players would say that they get their 'wages' in the cash games, whether live in the local casino, online or on a stop along the festival circuit. This is because you can choose who you play against, what the stakes are, and how long you play for – none of which are true in multi-table tournaments, where seating is random, the stakes are always rising and you must play until you win or go broke. Also, since you can usually choose the amount you sit down with (this is often capped online in big bet games) there is little

> **In multi-table tournaments seating is random, the stakes are always rising and you must play until you win or go broke**

contingency between the results of various pots, whereas in a big event your results for the entire month or year might be grouped around a series of crucial final-table hands. In a cash game, though, if someone gets lucky against you it's easy just to take out more money and try to get it back.

In deep water

Bankroll requirements vary wildly for cash depending on the type of game, and it takes an experienced player to know when they're out of their depth or need to drop down and recover in the smaller games. Obviously big-bet games need deeper pockets than limit ones, wild and short-handed ones offer more fluctuation than tight ring games and pot-limit Omaha players need bigger tanks than pot-limit hold'em ones who play at similar stakes.

The experts on limit hold'em often quote a bankroll of around 300 big bets for ring games, but in looser or short-handed games this number is probably too low. Similarly, for pot-limit and no-limit hold'em games you will need anywhere between 25 and 50 buy-ins, depending on the type of games you play, your style and the relation of your sit-down to the blinds, and for pot-limit Omaha you can probably double these numbers.

SIT&GOS

'Sit&gos', or small, fixed-field online tournaments, are an excellent way to learn cheaply, make some money, and to maximise a limited bankroll – they are also great practice for bigger final tables. You can choose to play heads-up, against four or five players, or in a one-, two- or three-table format, and the game will only start when the required number of players have registered.

Buy-ins and possibilities vary from site to site, but almost all have very low stakes games for beginners and the basic one-table tournament where nine or ten players enter and three get paid along a 50%, 30%, 20% structure.

You shark, them dinner

In terms of bankroll management and game selection these events score very highly indeed, for a variety of reasons. You can simply unregister if you don't like the field and, while an excellent player might only need to maintain a bankroll of 20 buy-ins to keep safely afloat, even a moderately skilled player shouldn't ever need more than 30. Because the buy-in is fixed, it's very easy to keep results and move up and down the various stakes as you see fit.

Furthermore, for the expert player sit&gos offer an attractive edge since, besides playing worse poker generally, more inexperienced players also tend to perform worse as games gets short-handed, when they fail to understand and employ a number of specialist tournament concepts which are vital for poker success.

TOURNAMENTS

Multi-table tournaments are probably the most frustrating, costly to the bankroll, and hardest to win consistently out of all formats of poker, but they also attract most of the new players as well as the cameras, headlines and the biggest prize pools. Make no mistake about it, though, in the immortal words of leading player Dave 'Devilfish' Ulliott: 'You need a shitload of money to play the tournament circuit', so wherever you play bear this in mind and find a few regular games in which you know you are a consistent winner and which will allow you a base for 'taking shots' at that big score.

Reality bites

The actual amount you would need to survive just playing multi-table tournaments is almost impossible to calculate accurately and playing these events exclusively for a living is strongly dissuaded. Even in sit&gos you must play hundreds of games to even have a vague idea of your overall win rate and skill level, and in terms of multi-table games this can extend into the thousands (ie years or decades of play), especially when events both online and live are now producing four-figure fields and buy-ins vary in size, clustering your overall results around the biggest and most populated events you play.

Because of this and the contingent, compound nature of tournament play, the difference between a good player and a great one is magnified to a huge degree. When flights, hotels, taxis and other expenses are factored in the net result is often that players can't make a living and go broke, or spend ages discovering they don't belong among the elite players for whom these events are viable ways of making serious cash.

So it's no surprise that even among top tournament players (including several former world champions) many have backers or go broke frequently, and most of the European name players have jumped at the

> For every Moneymaker winning $2.5 million there are literally thousands who contribute to their ticket without seeing any return

opportunity of sponsorship, indicating that this is the most realistic future for tournament poker.

SATELLITES

Satellites are smaller tournaments that offer tickets into bigger ones as prizes, and are found both online and live, and in single and multi-table formats. They have become more popular recently as most sites now offer satellites to major events with buy-ins and expenses included, and while amateurs are eager to emulate Chris Moneymaker in becoming an unknown who wins the World Series of Poker, even pros are attracted by the value they offer.

But beware – for every Moneymaker winning $2.5 million there are literally thousands who contribute to their ticket and those of the other qualifiers without seeing any return. From a bankroll perspective the lure of the parlay must also be approached with care, since the chances of a serious return are minimal. While getting into an event cheaply is great, it's unlikely that over all the satellites you play in the long term that you'll get your ticket for much less than half-price.

Banking on a seat

Which is why you often hear cries of 'So why not just win the money in a cash game then?' Sure, the reason for this is probably because you either end up with a seat or don't, but bear in mind that the satellite approach can make less sense than first appears. For example, some new players spend much of their poker time trying to qualify for big events rather than gradually moving up the ranks to the point where they could just buy-in anyway.

On the other hand, many places let you win more than one seat and take away the cash equivalent (or sell the seat), so for specialist satellite players there's an extra angle here. But bear in mind what the number of seats available does to your bankroll fluctuations – if, for example, there's one seat per six players in a multi-table event then this may be a much safer option than a similar non-satellite event, but if it's a sit&go with just a seat to the winner or a multi-table event where very few get rewarded you might want to think twice before getting in too deep. All these factors must be considered to maximise your success. ✱

vc⟩poker.com

"I love playing in tournaments at VC Poker. It's just like playing in the games you see on TV."

Johnny Aces AKA John Lim, 26 year old graphic designer from Manchester.

At VC Poker you'll find one of the widest selections of tournaments available anywhere on the web. With big money multi-table tournaments, fast-paced sit and go's and the chance to win fantastic poker trips through our satellite programme, you're guaranteed to find the tournament action that's perfect for you.

vcpoker.com

Victor Chandler

GET SERIOUS

If we still have your attention, chances are you're destined for monster pots, tournament fame or simply a lot of high-adrenaline fun. Read on for our top tips on advanced play

I f you've been reading this from cover to cover and have taken on board all of our advice, by now you'll be pretty adept at playing Texas hold'em. You'll have at your disposal many of the attributes that turn a moderate player into a good player. You'll know how to play which cards in which position, how to play pairs, what pot odds you're getting when you call a large raise, and how to bluff and exploit an opponent's obvious tells. You've probably picked up some excellent tournament skills to boot.

But now it's time to get serious. In this section, we'll teach you how to deal with that strange, unavoidable psychosis caused by being the victim of a bad beat, namely going 'on tilt' – our therapy will get you through it.

You'll also find out about poker 'maniacs'. There are broadly four types of poker player, summarised as tight-passive, loose-passive, tight-aggressive (the best players fall into this camp) and loose-aggressive. This last grouping are often described as poker maniacs and can be very difficult to play against, but here we show you how.

And why restrict your game to hold'em? Over the following pages, we teach you about another type of poker called Omaha. This isn't for novices: it tends to attract much stronger players who have honed all the requisite poker skills playing 'hold'em and then applied them to a whole new game. You'll find many Omaha tables online (on sites such as *vcpoker.com*), so why not get to grips with it?

If you've read, understood and enjoyed this book, you'll find yourself well on the way to becoming a good poker player. Who knows? One day soon you might find yourself sitting across the final table of the World Series of Poker main event, a $10,000 buy-in tournament, alongside the likes of Phil Ivey, Greg 'Fossilman' Raymer and others from among the world's great players. A lot of these guys started playing poker on the net, and qualified for the WSOP online, so it's not just some pipe dream – it really *could* be you.

JOKERS IN THE PACK

Don't be intimidated by the hyper-aggressive play of a poker maniac. **Nolan Dalla** tells you how to tame these wild cards – and turn a tidy profit

Picture this. A man brings a brown grocery sack to a game, takes a seat and then dumps the entire contents of the bag – $25,000 – onto the poker table into one big pile. Bundles of hundred-dollar bills tumble onto the green felt. The man has everyone in the game covered at least five times over.

The date is winter 1996, the place Resorts International, Atlantic City, the game pot-limit Texas hold'em. The man posts his $5 blind and is dealt a hand. What happens next defies the imagination. He becomes an instant legend in poker circles. He proceeds to raise on each successive round of betting. This wouldn't be unusual but for one crucial detail: he *never looks at his cards.*

The man is an eccentric, a gambler, a freak, a risk-taker, an oddball – and a godsend to any poker game. He is the quintessential maniac, playing without any fear of losing and seemingly lacking any regard for money. Incredibly, he wins a few hands early on and busts two players at the table before meeting his inevitable destiny. The $25,000 lasts 20 minutes. His fate sealed, the man toddles out of the casino, never to be seen nor heard of again.

While this was an extreme example of what a maniac does to a poker game, it epitomises the grave risk and tremendous upside potential of having a maniac sitting at the poker table. The maniac is certainly capable of breaking his opponent with a combination of good hands and reckless aggression. However, in the long run, the maniac always meets his doom when confronted with the appropriate counter-strategy – specifically designed to neutralise the maniac's hyper-aggressive tendencies. Crafting a counter-strategy to deal with maniacs is the intent of this article.

Major impacts of a maniac in the game

A maniac presents a unique set of challenges for any poker player. In fact, the maniac is not always at a disadvantage. For instance, a maniac might fare well in heads-up play against a passive opponent. In short-handed games with multiple passive opponents the maniac likely enjoys a significant edge.

General poker theory suggests there are four basic types of poker player:

1 Weak-tight players who play very few hands and surrender pots too easily **2** Tight-aggressive players who play few hands but bet strongly when involved in a pot **3** Loose-aggressive players who play many hands and bet strongly **4** Loose-passive players who play many hands but surrender pots too often.

But I would add another group of players: **5** Maniacs. They deserve a special category all to themselves. What separates maniacs from loose-aggressive players is that maniacs play even more hands and tend to bet, raise, and re-raise to the point where the game is played for significantly higher stakes. Therefore, the dynamics of an ordinary poker game are altered radically because of the presence of the maniac. In short, a maniac usually displays the following characteristics and tendencies:

● He has more than an average number of chips on the table
● He often posts a live straddle (when permitted to do so)
● He plays far more hands than normal
● He raises and re-raises far more often than normal
● He bluffs far more often than normal

The maniac's demise usually comes in full-ring games (with at least eight players), where he is up against just one or two opponents in each hand – at least one of which (or even both) holds a stronger hand. What happens is that all the players become more disciplined and tend to play technically-correct poker. They wait for strong starting hands with which to confront the maniac. Hence, the maniac often faces the one or two best hands at the table, and is frequently at a disadvantage. Because opponents see that the maniac plays many hands and will pay the bets off with a flurry of raises, all that is necessary is to patiently wait for strong cards and let the odds work against the maniac.

Unfortunately, this poses a serious problem if you fail to get good starting hands. Some undisciplined players see chips flying around the table and can't contain themselves. They begin relaxing their own starting-hand requirements.

> **All that is necessary is to patiently wait for strong cards and let the odds work against the maniac**

These undisciplined players see the maniac occasionally win with garbage, and react by betting or raising with marginal cards. This plays right into the maniac's intent – to generate action, put opponents on tilt, and create a wild poker game with multiple players in every hand with huge pots.

Most games with a maniac usually fall into one of two categories – they are either very tight (two- or three-way action in most pots) or very wild (multiple opponents calling raises in every hand). The maniac's behaviour causes every single player at the table to adjust his strategy.

Basic strategy playing against a maniac

Keep in mind that in poker, seating position is absolutely critical. It is almost always advantageous to sit to a maniac's immediate left. The worst seat at the table is usually to the maniac's immediate right. So, in such a situation your first goal should be to select a favourable seat. Request a seat-change if possible. ➤

DEALING WITH A MANIAC
BASIC STRATEGIC CONCEPTS

How to exploit a maniac's weaknesses whatever type of game you're in...

In tight games (two- or three-way action in most hands)
- Play very tight in early position
- Play tight-aggressive in late position
- Check and call and/or check-raise more often, since the maniac will usually bet when checked to
- Induce bluffs and tend to call more often. Call-down the maniac's bets and raises, even when holding a marginal hand
- Don't attempt to bluff

In standard games (four- or five-way action in most hands)
- Play tight in early position
- Play aggressively in late position

- Re-raise more often, in an attempt to isolate the maniac and get heads-up
- Call down the maniac's bets and raises more often, even when holding a marginal hand
- Don't attempt to bluff

In wild games (six-way action or more in most hands)
- Play suited-connectors, pairs, and Ace-suited hands more often
- Check and call when pot odds dictate there is value
- Throw away marginal hands when other players have raised or re-raised
- Don't attempt isolation moves (for instance, re-raising pre-flop) since most opponents are likely to just call anyway
- Don't attempt to bluff

> With a maniac in the game, the ultimate objective is to get in with the best hand, anticipating that the maniac will pay off on all bets and raises. In tight games, a tight-aggressive play is usually the optimal strategy. In other words, in hold'em enter a pot with premium starting hands (pairs higher than 7-7 and non-pairs like A-K and A-Q), and bet them aggressively. The maniac will often try to intimidate you into folding by raising and re-raising. But since you are playing good cards more often than not, you will end up with the best hand and win more pots.

In wild games, a very different strategy is necessary. Since the maniac has created multi-way action and big pots, drawing hands increase significantly in value. Pre-flop hands like suited-connectors, small pairs, and Ace-suited are often playable cards. If you have two suited cards and flop two cards to your suit, a raise by the maniac actually increases your expected value in the hand, since you will win a much bigger pot when you make the flush (which happens about 37% of the time when you flop a flush draw).

Check out our Dealing With A Maniac box above for more basic strategic concepts when playing against a maniac.

Differences between limit and no-limit games with a maniac at the table

So far, most of the strategic concepts discussed relate to limit hold'em games. However, pot-limit and no-limit games present their own unique circumstances.

It's important to note that maniacs can dominate a big-money game, especially when stoked with big bankrolls against timid opponents. Players who are afraid to lose their chips fall victim to the maniac's hyper-aggressive tendencies. In a sense, they get run over. Once the maniac discovers this weakness, he simply launches raise after

raise at his helpless opponent, and more often than not will win pot after pot – even though he likely doesn't have the best hand. Such dynamics are simply not possible in limit hold'em games, since the amount of betting is fixed on each round and opponents are less likely to be intimidated by the size of the wager.

This concept is important because it's essential to accept the reality that bankroll swings in pot-limit and no-limit hold'em games will be much more severe with a maniac at the table. In pot-limit and no-limit games it is far more difficult to 'find out where you are at' – to use a common poker expression – with a bet or raise when facing a maniac.

For example, with a strong but vulnerable hand such as Q-Q, it is probably best to throw your hand away when you bet out and are raised by an opponent after an Ace flops. In a conventional game, the opponent is likely to have an Ace, which means you are beat. But when a manic raises in this situation, you are forced to play a guessing game, which is not a good position to be in.

Poker is as much about psychology as card values. It's important to try and understand why the maniac plays so recklessly

The long and the short of it is that it's tough to play against maniacs in pot-limit and no-limit games when contrasted with fixed-limit games.

Keep the maniac happy while you fleece him

Poker is just as much a game of psychology as it is of card values. Accordingly, there are several specific tactics which can be used to keep the maniac sitting in the game for longer periods of time, and therefore steadily contributing to your profits at the table.

Most maniacs are losing poker players. Over the long run there's no way that maniacal behaviour can bring in a decent profit. No amount of talent or experience can overcome playing way too many hands and putting one's money into the pot repeatedly with the worst hand. So, it's important to try and understand why the maniac plays so recklessly. Does he simply like to gamble? Is he a wealthy eccentric playing for insignificant stakes? Or does the attention he receives at the table stroke his ego? There are a myriad of reasons for maniacal behaviour, and identifying the underlying cause of such behaviour is the first step towards exploiting it for profit.

Whatever the root causes may be, most maniacs – indeed, most poker players – want to enjoy themselves at the table. It's human nature. Disparaging remarks and negative comments made by so-called pros towards these players are incredibly detrimental to both the short- and long-term winnings that might be gained from having maniacs in the game. It's an important point to remember.

It might sound dubious, but believe me, the ultimate counter-strategy when you're playing poker with a maniac is to let the player think he can dominate a game, and that you – his opponent – can be manipulated at the table. Letting the maniac think he can run over you and bully you into losing, while you are actually prepared to confront his aggressiveness with proper counter-strategies, effectively sets the perfect trap. In essence, the maniac has committed the very worst error of poker – underestimating his opponent. ✿

TILTING AT POKER WINDMILLS

Fail to cope with luck's inevitable fluctuations and you career crazily on tilt, making deluded plays that only compound your losses. **Phil Shaw** explains how to avoid becoming poker's Don Quixote

As a game of both luck and skill, poker can offer limitless moneymaking opportunities, but it can also be a rollercoaster ride of ups and downs that pushes your abilities and nerves to their limits. The aim of this article is to talk you through the swings that poker players should expect to encounter every time they play, and to explain how you can stay away from the dreaded four letter word that has busted many a bankroll – 'tilt'.

Poker is an alluring mixture of luck and skill that makes for an exciting experience, whether you're playing or just watching. The really great thing about it compared to, say, chess, snooker or even football, is that for limited periods of time *anyone* can win. We see newcomers beating pros or triumphing at big tournaments and walking off with huge prizes. Contrast that with other games and sports – the vast majority of us could only ever dream of emulating Ronnie O'Sullivan or David Beckham.

But, if you've played poker for any length of time, then you'll be aware that the downside is that you can get extremely unlucky for seemingly extraordinary periods of time,

perhaps weeks or even months, and you will never really reach an even keel, as the swings go back and forth continuously.

Whatever level of involvement in poker you decide upon – from weekly home game to full-time pro – your nerves and abilities are going to be tested, and perhaps pushed beyond their limits at various points in your playing career when things go badly. Of course, if things go better than average then your main problem might be an inflated ego and estimation of your abilities, which can also be a problem as things start to even out!

Working out the angles
Coping with the fluctuations in your luck then is a vital part of the game and, as all poker players know, what happens when you don't manage this is called 'tilt' – ie playing one or more hands incorrectly due to external pressures (often associated with bad beats earlier in a game), and thereby compounding your losses through bad luck with additional ones through bad play.

This is one of the most costly 'leaks' a poker player can have, and has sent many a player broke or out of a tournament unnecessarily.

In fact it's so prevalent that almost no player is completely immune to going on tilt, but the best all manage to keep a handle on it, or just stop playing for a while if it's affecting their game. So how do you keep yourself on the straight and narrow, and off tilt?

Tilt is a four letter word, and like most four letter words it can usually be associated with an occurrence that's not to our liking, or beyond our normal expectations of what is reasonable. In poker these kind of occurrences come up all the time, whether it's a donkey (read: bad player) calling you down with a terrible hand in a limit hold'em game and hitting a two outer, or losing a long series of coin-flip hands in no-limit tournament play.

This is partly because the odds of losing are never massive in most poker situations compared to winning the lottery or getting struck by lightning, and partly because the uneven swings always guarantee there will be times when you're getting far fewer good hands

> **No player is completely immune to going on tilt, but the best all manage to keep a handle on it, or just stop playing for a while**

than you would usually and taking far more than your share of beats as well. This makes for a serious shock to the system because somehow our brains are hardwired to believe we're entitled to win every 3/1 shot, and to glide over the good luck we have (most of which we never even see since players usually fold their cards face down), rather than rationalise it and accept it as being the same for everyone.

Take a wage cut
One important reason for this goes back to the unstable nature of the game, and thereby a player's results – serious poker students and pros keep records of their wins and losses to know where they are overall, and a bad run can leave a crater in your overall expectation per hour or per game, thereby affecting the overall estimation of projected profits severely, as well as a player's confidence levels. Just imagine the boss coming into your office every other day to tell you your wage has just doubled or halved!

IN THE FAMILY
EXPLAINING POKER TO FAMILY AND FRIENDS

Get your family on side so you can concentrate on playing your best and staying off tilt

Poker can sometimes become a sticking point with others to whom it may appear that you're wasting time and money 'gambling'. Of course this isn't the case, as poker isn't anything like craps or roulette and the talented young guns of today's poker world are more acquainted with PlayStation than Pai-Gow.

But how do you explain this to friends, family and partner? Start with the example of tossing coins, keeping some chips on hand to track the flow of the game. Illustrate with a few spins and an even-money bet (ie if you win the spin you get one chip and vice versa) that this is a 'break even proposition', and that even if after a dozen or so spins if one of you is ahead then your 'equity' on the game is zero – in the long run you stand to neither lose nor gain.

Flip it to them
Now tell your inductee that for every spin they win you'll give them two chips, but if they win then they only have to give you one. Try a few more spins until they get the message that overall they're going to win significantly. Then explain this is the essence of winning at poker – making good bets, and refusing bad ones. Of course, if it was for money you'd never offer someone 2/1 on a coin flip, but with poker many people play for fun or don't know the maths so continually lay and take the wrong odds, giving you – the poker student – the opportunity to profit.

Sticking with the 2/1 coin-flipping example, and ask them how much they'd bet over hundreds of hands, relative to their net worth in terms of possessions and savings. If they owned £100,000, how much would they bet per hand – £100, £1,000, £10,000? Certainly it would be a profitable bet, and the more profitable, the higher the amount wagered – plus some people are happier to take risks than others. But what would be the right amount to wager mathematically to maximise profits, without going bankrupt or, as gamblers say, 'broke'?

Then relate this example to the idea of 'bankroll', or as a non-poker player sees it, the money you gamble with and refuse to spend or lend to them. Because, like your overall net worth in the example, your bankroll should define what games you can and can't afford to play without going broke, and the bigger it is, the more you can potentially make from playing in bigger games. So, if they force you to cut down on your reserves, the flow of gifts and holidays could soon dry up too – and they wouldn't want that, would they? Sorted!

➤ Having said that though, the main way of rationally combating tilt from such bad runs is to realise that while there's little you can do about the fluctuations in your luck, the bad beats you experience are actually the cornerstone of the game – after all, if bad players never got lucky they probably wouldn't play in the first place, and if you're one of the best players in your game it makes sense that you will be taking more bad beats than others.

If you want to take the idea one step further, imagine that you're running a business. To run a healthy business you need to keep the bank manager happy, and so a key factor is having enough money behind you to keep from worrying about going broke. It also helps to have the support of those close to you in such endeavours, and so see our boxout on the left to help with this.

Stake and chips
Having looked at the reasons behind tilt and how to rationalise the swings in a poker game, you should now be in a good position to stay off it. But just in case that wasn't enough, here are a final few practical questions you can ask to stop yourself going on tilt when you're in a game or thinking about sitting down in one:

How are you feeling? Any sort of emotional cloud could affect your game, whether it's due to a relationship, work issues or a previous bad run that had affected your confidence. In poker, like anywhere else, pessimism can be a self-fulfilling prophecy, so

> **If bad players never got lucky they wouldn't play, and if you're one of the best players, you'll be taking more bad beats than others**

if you don't feel able to crush the game (or at least eke out a modest profit) stand up or give it a miss altogether – especially on the internet, there's always another when you're up to it. At times like this a calming walk in the park or trip to the cinema would probably be a better idea

Get a grip on yourself
Are you in good shape to play? Just as emotions are a factor, what about the rest of you? If you've played a long session already or are tired from something else, your judgement and emotional control can begin to falter, which can be doubly perilous. Similarly, being ill or drunk are good reasons to not get involved over your head, and if you're losing focus and starting to resent or pick battles with other players for the sake of it you're probably not at your best.

Can you afford to play? It's an obvious but important question. The biggest hidden factor in tilt is the stakes you're playing at. For example, playing in a bigger game than you're used to can result in playing fearfully or skidding down the slopes to disaster if you get off to a bad start. Playing in a game that is too small for you might result in you not taking enough care with it.

Usually, but not always, this is related to an overall sense of financial pressure based on the size of your bankroll, as it's hard to focus effectively when every hand means an immediate threat to your survival. Sure, you can take a shot at a favourable bigger game in an effort to move up limit, but be careful to get out early if things go wrong or you'll start to feel the pressure! ❈

vc poker.com

Live the challenge.

Nothing beats that winning feeling. And thanks to the huge range of tournaments that run every single day at VC Poker, you've got plenty of chances to get used to it.

From big money multi-table events to freerolls and heads-up challenges, we don't only offer choice, we offer value too. Catch the tournament bug at VC Poker and take up the challenge today.

Victor Chandler

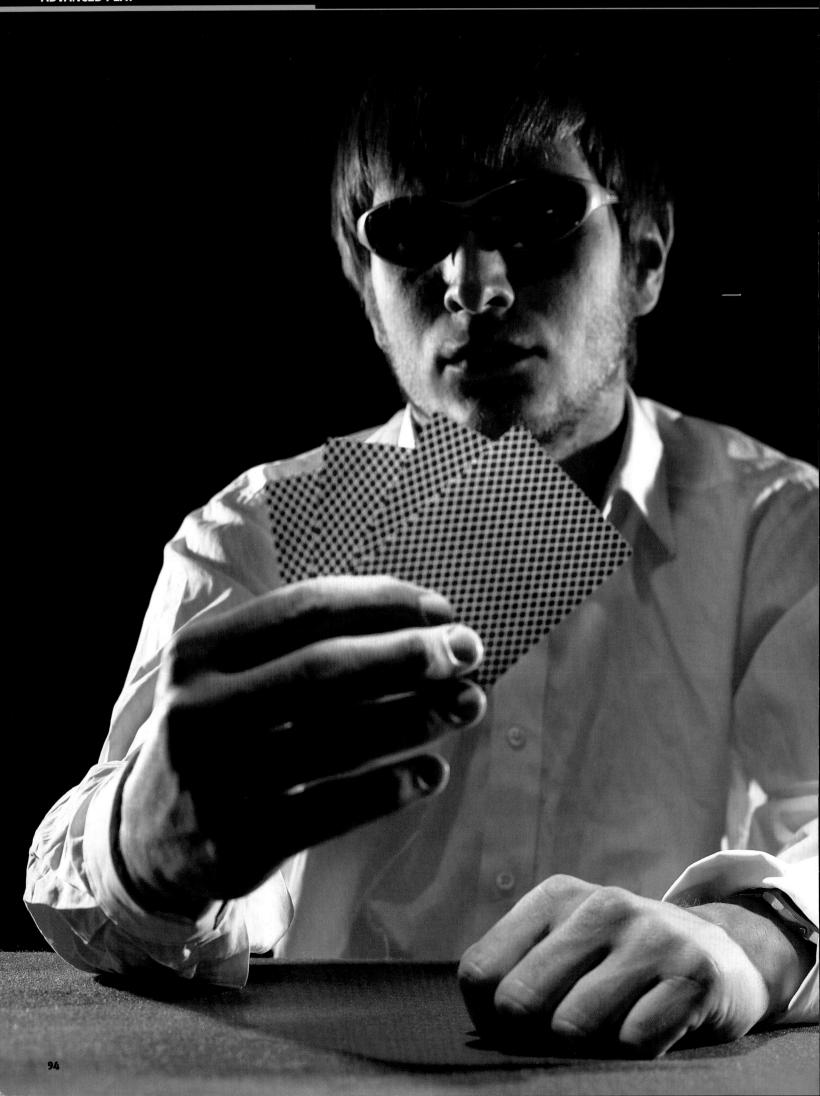

LET GO OF HOLD'EM AND
HEAD FOR OMAHA

Many Texas hold'em players are trying their hands at Omaha, but their assumption that they can make the leap easily is often their undoing. So how do you avoid looking like a tenderfoot when you make the switch?

At first glance, taking up Omaha when you already understand Texas hold'em seems easy – just a case of moving from a five-community-card game with two hole cards to a five-community-card game with four hole cards.

Yet just as first glances at members of the opposite sex and their apparent attractiveness has led most of us into trouble at one time or another, so too has the hold'em player's first lustful glance at Omaha. They're lulled into a false sense of security by their hard-won hold'em knowledge – all too often their understanding of hand values and what's important in the game leads them to incorrect conclusions in Omaha.

Omaha is played in both high-only and high-low (with an 8-low qualifier) versions. For reasons that will make sense after you've been playing Omaha for a long time, no-limit Omaha has never really caught on. Pot-limit Omaha, the game with the unfortunate initials (PLO), is certainly the most popular form of high-stakes Omaha. Omaha 8-or-better is probably the most popular form of low-stakes Omaha.

The exponential pot-sized betting increases involved in PLO make it enormously different from limit Omaha. The difference is even more pronounced than one sees between limit hold'em and pot-limit hold'em, because so many more reasonable hands can be played for raises. Those differences, combined with PLO's popularity, require us to examine both PLO and the limit variations when comparing Omaha to hold'em.

Let's now get into the key differences in the two games, starting with the most important:

1 THE 'MUST TWO' RULE

In hold'em, a player can use one, two or none of his hole cards to create his final hand – if there's a royal flush on the board, every single player in the pot at the end will receive an equal share of the pot.

But in Omaha you *must* use two – and *only* two – of your four hole cards in forming your final five-card poker hand. This rule leads to all kinds of curious situations. In hold'em, you would love to look at your two hole cards and see two Aces. In Omaha, if your four hole cards are the four Aces (or any four of a kind), you essentially have a 'must fold' hand (unless, perhaps, you are playing heads-up), because you have a pair of Aces and no way whatsoever to improve them. You can't make a flush or a straight – you must use two of those Aces – and clearly another Ace can't hit the board.

Indeed, most hands that contain just three of a kind are completely unplayable, although in a high-only game you might consider trying A♠-A♥-A♦-K♦ (a pair of aces and one nut flush draw) from the small blind in a multi-way limp pot, and in high-low you could also play A♠-A♥-A♦-2♦ because you would almost certainly hold the only A-2 (you'd also have one nut flush draw, and while your pair of Aces doesn't add much to your equity, you would be the only player who could hold a pair of Aces).

I vividly remember the first time I played Omaha, in a private game about 25 years ago. The final board showed K♥-Q♦-10♣-K♣-Q♥. I had an A-J in my hand, so I had a straight, and I called at the showdown. My opponent, a friend in a friendly game (even though the stakes were £10-£20), held up a lone card, a King, and I tossed my hand towards the muck.

'What's your other card, Eddie?' asked a more experienced player who knew full well it was my first time out. Eddie showed an Ace, meaning he had three Kings with an Ace kicker, and not the full house I was accustomed to that King meaning in hold'em. I protested that I'd held a straight, and because this was a friendly game, Eddie actually gave me half the pot. I'd been 'entitled' to all of it, of course, but if ➤

In Omaha you *must* use two – and *only* two – of your four hold cards in forming your final five-card hand

◄ You must use two of your hole cards to make your hand. Here the Jack and the 8 can be used to make up the low end of a straight. Anyone with a Jack and a King would beat you

◄ You should make sure all your hole cards work together. Although not a great hand, the A♦ is supported by a 6♦ and 5♦, which could be used to make the nut flush

◄ Pocket Aces in Omaha are not that powerful, especially if they aren't supported. Only the A♦ is supported by a 10♦ and the 7♠ is nothing more than a 'dangler'

➤ you muck your hand in any kind of serious game, what you're entitled to doesn't matter.

This is why it's vitally important to 'table' your hand (place all four cards face up on the table, without mucking them) in any situation where you're not completely sure what you hold. Once you table your hand, other players and the dealer are entitled to help you read it. This assistance often pays dividends, and there's nothing to be ashamed of. I have seen players at the final table of a World Series of Poker event staring at the same Omaha hand, all trying to figure out what the hand's owner has!

The 'must two' rule means:

● You cannot 'play the board.' You can only play three-fifths of it
● You cannot play a single card from your hand (the 'Eddie rule,' as I have come to call it)
● You cannot play three or four cards from your hand
● Just because there are four suited cards on board and multiple players in the hand, it isn't a 'lock' that someone has a flush, because 'someone' will have to hold two cards in suit, not just one.

You must get accustomed to thinking of your Omaha hole cards not as individual cards but as six possible combinations of two cards

You must get accustomed to thinking of your Omaha hole cards not as individual cards, but as groups of two. With four cards in your hand, you hold six possible two-card combinations. A strong Omaha hand gets equity or value from as many of these six combinations as possible – ideally, significant value from all six.

2 POSITION IS LESS IMPORTANT

Good hold'em players know that position – playing on or as near to the button as possible – is vitally important to winning play, so much so that many hands worth a raise in late position are not even worth a call in early position. In Omaha, position isn't irrelevant, but it pales in comparison to hand values. It would be fair to say that hold'em is a game of position, while Omaha is a game of card combinations. Why is this so? It's because…

3 WINNING HANDS TEND TO BE STRONGER

Even though every once in a while the 'must two' rule will devalue a hand, as in the 'Eddie' situation, where his solitary King didn't give him the full house it would have in hold'em, over the long haul, the typical winning hand is much stronger in Omaha than it is in hold'em. The reason is obvious: instead of only one two-card combination that can be used together with the board, the player has six such combinations possible from his four cards. Someone playing A♥-K♥-J♦-9♠ and staring at a flop of Q♥-8♥-2♠ may be focused almost entirely on his nut heart flush draw, but if a 10 hits the board, the player has made a straight with his J-9 combination.

Good Omaha players don't focus entirely on one part of their hand. They examine all the little bits and pieces of equity that each of the combinations represent. This is one of the reasons why you may have heard the expression 'Don't play Omaha hands containing a dangler.' A dangler is one card that doesn't work together well with the other three cards in your hand.

For example, if you hold K-Q-J-10, your cards all work together well. The six combinations will give you a straight with almost any combination of high cards on the board. If instead you held K-Q-J-2, the deuce is a dangler. While it could help (if, say, the flop comes 2-2-4, which is still a pretty vulnerable hand), it's far

less valuable than a card that adds to the straight possibilities, because Omaha tends to be a game of straights, flushes, and full houses – at least at low stakes, where many players stay in, or in PLO, if the pot is going to grow very large.

Hold'em players are accustomed to hands like top pair, top kicker being strong (for example, holding A-Q and getting a flop of Q, 5, 4). In Omaha, top pair, top kicker is practically useless, unless you're only sat down with one, two or – at a push – three other players. Even then, you shouldn't be raising or even calling big bets with it.

Indeed, in games where many people see the flop, a good rule of thumb is to assume that if a hand is possible, someone either has it or is drawing to it. When only two or three players see the flop this isn't true, but with six people in, players are trying to match 24 cards up with the flop (36 two-card combinations). Good Omaha players, in multi-way pots, play hands that are either the nuts or a draw to the nuts.

4 ONCE YOU'VE MADE YOUR HAND, YOU STILL OFTEN NEED TO IMPROVE TO WIN

Omaha is said to be a game of draws and redraws. Suppose, for example, that you hold K♥-Q♥-10♣-10♠, and you get a great flop: 10♥, 5♥, 4♥. You've flopped a flush, although you need to beware, because it's not the nut flush. You have also flopped top set. Although three 10s isn't as strong a hand as your King-high flush, the set gives you a redraw to a full house.

Should a 4 land on the turn, you now have the top full house, and only need to worry about someone who has quad 4s (quads occur much more frequently in Omaha, although in a high-only game, it isn't as likely that someone would hold a low pair like fours, because small sets can be just as costly as non-nut flushes) or someone who held either the 7♥-6♥ or the 3♥-2♥ (giving him a straight flush draw).

Even though they do appear more often in Omaha then in hold'em, you can't live in fear of quads and straight flushes. If you make the top full house, you should bet it strongly, and only if your pot-sized re-raise gets re-raised by a strong player should you slow down and consider that you might be up against four of a kind (in limit poker, you should probably put in four raises before you decide just to call).

PLO pots can grow rather quickly, and while a weak opponent might make a big raise with a lesser full house and a strong one might make it to apply money pressure, sometimes discretion is the better part of valour. In hold'em, quads are so rare that you can almost always be excused for going broke when you face them; in Omaha, you need to at least consider the possibility once you face a third or fourth raise.

Whether you're playing PLO or straight limit, your work isn't done when you've flopped a good hand. It's usually important to have some kind of draw to something better. You may not need to improve, but it's the equity you get from these redraws that can turn a losing session into a winner.

5 IT'S EASIER TO GET SUCKED INTO PLAYING WEAK HANDS

Hold'em players will often get exasperated during a losing stretch and start playing garbage cards, chanting the Loser's Lament: 'Any two cards can win,' but most players of any ability won't continue to play hands like J♥-2♥ ('But it was suited!') for very long.

In Omaha, the saying, 'Any four cards can win' comes much closer to the truth. It may seem hard to believe, but in a heads-up situation, there are *very* few Omaha starting hands that are even 2/1 favourites over a random opponent hand.

Naturally, you can construct scenarios where one starting hand is a much bigger favourite than that: if you give your opponent 2♥-2♠-2♣-2♦, he isn't going to win very often! But if you assume your opponent has a random and weak-looking collection of cards like J♠-8♣-5♦-3♥, even a magnificent starting hand like A♦-A♣-J♦-10♣ is only about 2/1 favourite. Your opponent can make various straights and flushes that you cannot, can make numerous two-pair combinations that you cannot, and is going to get five community cards to try to make

something out of his mess of a hand.

Because the random hands *do* have a reasonable chance of winning, many bad or tilted Omaha players get sucked into playing bad hands more often than their hold'em counterparts. While the results on any given Omaha hand are going to be better, over the long-term, the results are just as certain.

You don't even have to start playing garbage hands like J♠-8♣-5♦-3♥ to get into trouble. Just playing hands with danglers is bad enough. Play A♠-K♠-Q♦-6♠ often enough, and that almost completely useless 6 will send you home a loser against people who play hands where all the cards work together, even if their first three aren't as impressive as your first three.

A lengthy discussion of the best Omaha starting hands goes beyond this article's scope, but A♦-A♣-J♦-10♣ is my example of a magnificent hand. Some people have other favorites – right there you see a significant difference in the games, because no one debates A-A's value as the best hold'em starting hand.

A strong Omaha high hand will include the following elements:

- High cards
- Cards that connect up well for straight purposes
- Cards that give you nut flush draws
- Cards that give you the chance to make full houses or quads

A♦-A♣-J♦-10♣ gives you a pair that can make the best full house or quads, two nut-flush draws, multiple combinations for high straights, and the single two-card combination (J-10) that makes more straights than any other two-card combination. Some people argue for hands like A♦-A♣-K♦-Q♣ (sacrificing a few straights for a few more high

Because random hands do have a reasonable chance of winning, many bad or tilted players get sucked into playing bad hands more often

pairs), but it's one of those pleasant choices that isn't going to make or break your day, because you'll play them both the same: very hard before the flop and not at all after the flop, unless they coordinate well with it.

6 KNOW YOUR OUTS

We've already mentioned that position is far less important in Omaha than in hold'em, due to the comparative strength of the hands. This means your ability to calculate pot odds and possible outs (cards that can improve your hand over your opponents') are deadly weapons in the Omaha player's arsenal. In fact, your mental arithmetic will need to be top-notch if you want to become a killer Omaha player.

If, like most people, you're playing Omaha online, you're also going to be short of tells and useful information, so your maths skills become even more important.

Say, for example, that you start with A♠-K♠-7♥-6♥ and the flop comes J♠, 4♠, 5♦. At the moment, your hand is worthless and a pot raise probably indicates someone holding three Jacks, the current nuts. However, there are lots of ways you can improve, so you need to be able to calculate your outs. Beginning with any spade will give you the nut flush, so that gives you a total of nine outs (there are 13 cards in a suit, two are on the board and you hold two, so there are up to nine remaining in the deck). Then any 3 or any 8 will give you the nut straight. This means another six outs (there are four 3s and four 8s available, but one of each of these will be spades so you can't double-count them). As a result, on this flop you have 15 outs.

As a rule of thumb, each out equates to about a 4% chance to improve, so ➤

THE LAW OF THE DRAW
STRATEGY IN ACTION

Omaha is a game of draws and redraws. But even the most powerful of hands can be rendered useless by a random flop...

AT LAST! A great hand – Aces double suited with loosely connected cards. My position isn't great so I must make a pot-sized raise to ensure I'm not taking on everyone...

MY PRE-FLOP RAISE works and I now have position and just one player left in. Unfortunately, the flop misses by a mile – my hand is still nothing more than a pair of Aces...

THE RIVER and the turn bring nothing but my aces hold! Any bet from the other player and the Aces would've hit the muck as even a weak two pair would be dominating

◄ Although this hand may look pretty good, I will need a Q or a 10 on the flop to make it worth betting hard. There's also an outside chance that it could make a straight or a weak flush in spades

◄ Bluff with caution in Omaha. After a checked flop and a weak bet, I come over the top with a pot raise holding no more than two pair. As it is, the bluff is called...

◄ Mid-pairs can spell real trouble in Omaha. If you hit your set they can often make up a full house that is easily dominated by higher pairs. Play with caution!

➤ you have a 60% chance of improving your hand. Good odds, you might think and well worth calling – but don't forget that your opponent, who is probably sitting on trip Jacks, will have outs to improve as well. He can hit any pair to make a full house (that's six outs or a Jack to make quads, another out). As such, you need to subtract his seven outs from your 15 and you have the right odds for playing a pot and winning it uncontested. Suddenly you only have a one in four chance of winning this pot with the best hand. Whether you call will depend on the size of the bet you have to call and what's in the pot that you can win.

You also need to work through the same exercise on the turn. If the turn draws a relative blank – 10♦, say – then you need to re-calculate. You would now have another three outs (any Queen except Q♦) to make the nut straight. Look again at the total board: J♦, 4♦, 5♦, 10♦. If your opponent's hand is J♣-J♦-9♦-Q♣, then this turn card will have greatly improved their hand. Any diamond will give them a flush, and the 8 you needed for your straight will now give them a better straight – proving Omaha really is a game of redraws!

If you can master the ability to assess how your hand connects with the flop and how you can improve, it becomes hard to lose money

This may seem laborious and complex, but the ability to calculate these kind of odds on the fly separates winning Omaha players from mediocre ones. If you can master the ability to assess how your hand connects with the flop and how you can improve, it becomes very hard to lose money at Omaha in the long run.

7 BET IT HARD

With draws being so key to Omaha, it's critical that you don't let other players make draws cheaply or for free. If you have top trips or the nut flush, make sure you make pot-sized bets and re-raises where you can. This applies to both the flop and especially to the turn, where you can really make other players pay just to see the remaining card. Pot-limit games also benefit you here, as the pot will be at least three times the size by the turn (if you make a max raise followed by a call). Don't lose your bottle if you still hold the nuts on the turn, as it's always painful to see the board pair when you're holding the nuts or see a potential flush made when you're holding trips. In short, bet your hands as hard and aggressively as your opponent will allow.

My advice is never to slow-play a hand, except when you have an absolute monster. Monsters include quads (where you hope someone else will make the nut full house by waiting) or a straight or royal flushes.

The only other situation where you don't want to overbet your hand is with a nut straight and no chance of improving. As a rule of thumb, two out of three straights will be overturned in an internet game of Omaha. For instance, you hold J♣-10♣-4♣-3♦ and the flop is 7♣, 8♣, 9♥. You currently have the nuts so make an early-position pot raise. Another player raises and then a further player re-raises! You have the nuts! However, there's every chance another player does, too, but has a hand that could improve – for example, 10♥-J♥-A♣-Q♣. They have the upside of the straight and a nut flush draw; or perhaps J♥-J♣-10♣-10♥. They have a full-house draw and a mid-flush draw. Either way, you want to get out of the hand. Even if your straight does hold up, you'll probably end up sharing the pot anyway. Painful as it may seem, with two other players in the pot, this is one nut-hand you should choose to fold as you simply can't improve.

8 KNOW WHERE YOU STAND

When your mind is spinning with pot odds, outs and redraws, you can sometimes miss the obvious. This means missing what you actually have in your hand and what draws you can make. Sites such as VC Poker show your current best hand, which definitely helps. However, make sure you know what the nuts is at every stage. It can be all too easy to bet the nut straight hard, missing that the river delivered the third suit necessary for a flush.

9 YOU NEED THE NUTS

The classic hold'em player's mistake in Omaha is to over-value hands; dynamite hands in hold'em can be little more than damp squibs in Omaha.

The worst of these is a weaker full house (sometimes called the underhouse), as these can be extremely costly. If you flop two pairs, especially if they're mid-pairs, your hand is next to useless if you have more than one player left in the hand.

Even if you make your full house, it's likely to be beaten. The same goes for mid and low pairs. If you hold 8♥-8♣-7♥-6♦ and the flop comes K♣, K♠, 8♦, you currently have a pretty strong full house. Anyone holding a King will probably call a pot raise and then the turn comes a Queen, and suddenly you could easily be losing (in fact, even someone left in with Q-Q will now beat you). Remember that Kings full of anything will beat you. Play mid pairs with extreme caution.

As an aside, I prefer playing with small pairs (5-5 suited and below). This is because if they quad up, you can make some massive pots from players with A-A suited and K-K suited who hold what they think are unbeatable full houses. At the same time, their obvious weakness means there's never any temptation to overplay them. Low pairs can be profitable starting hands if you can limp into pots cheaply.

It goes without saying that non-nut flushes – even King high – aren't much use in Omaha, despite being mighty in hold'em. Further, bottom straights are worth very little – if you own the ignorant end of a straight you should call only the smallest of bets on the river, if at all.

Except for quads, it's always a good rule of thumb to assume you're facing the nuts in Omaha, especially in multi-way pots, so...

10 BLUFF WITH EXTREME CAUTION

Since most good players are playing with or drawing to the nuts, making a successful bluff in Omaha needs the right sort of board and a good instinct on the betting pattern.

Most bluffs are best played on the turn when the board pairs and the betting pattern indicates a straight or a flush. Just remember that a bluff will have to be a large or pot-sized bet to push someone off their hand, so bluffing in Omaha isn't a strategy for the faint-hearted.

The flipside of this is that big raises in Omaha are very rarely bluffs, so respect them: you'll be facing the nuts nine out of ten times.

Other bluffs can be constructed before you have even seen a flop. If you have the button and the bets limp around to you, a pot-sized bet can give you the pot then and there, or perhaps one or two callers at worst. If the latter is the case and any high cards hit on the flop, a pot raise allows you to represent trips very easily if the bet is checked around to you. Only the bravest or the most foolish players will call with weak draws and only the cleverest will see the bluff and re-raise.

11 OMAHA IS A NUMBERS GAME

Okay, so we know that maths and pot-odds rule the roost in Omaha. This means that Omaha is a far less 'lucky' game than hold'em and that, although miracle outs will always hit, beginners will get eaten alive by experienced players.

This fact probably explains why Omaha will never be as popular as hold'em. With a few good cards, a complete novice can break a professional hold'em player and carry on winning for quite some time. In Omaha, however, gamblers who draw to non-nut hands or look for case cards and gutshot draws will quickly be bankrupted.

If you do get beaten by a miracle one-outer, it's also easier to deal with in Omaha. After all, the odds were with you and you wanted that bet called. It doesn't make the call any less expensive, just that much easier to deal with!

Omaha isn't – at least superficially – a more skilful game than hold'em, but you do need different skills to be a winner. However, the complexity of bluffing and the psychology of hold'em probably does make it the more skilful game *in the long-run*.

12 IT'S HARDER TO HOLD YOUR CARDS!

This might seem silly, but it's true. Almost anyone can squeeze two hold'em cards and keep them hidden from his neighbour, but it's not as easy when you're holding four cards.

You actually need to practice holding your cards in a manner where you can see them and your opponents can't. Omaha players are quite accustomed to getting free looks at their neighbours' cards, simply because they hold them up like a five-card draw hand to see them.

While on the subject of holding your cards, it's also important either to have a perfect memory for suits – something most of us lack – or to be willing to check back at your hand to see if you are suited there when two flush cards hit the flop.

Because this is a signal that *if* you're suited it's almost certainly not with a suited Ace (players remember when they have suited Aces), if you do need to go back and look at your cards you also need to do it on hands even when you know perfectly well that you hold the A♠-10♠. If you're playing a long session with the same players, or playing a game with regulars, your opponent who holds K♠-Q♠ will only need one stinging reminder that you'll

check your cards again even with a suited Ace – he won't take your glance back as a tell ever again.

If you're lucky enough to find a live Omaha game, then you need to be comfortable with four cards, not the usual two.

In conclusion

Learning to play Omaha to a high level takes a long time, just like any form of poker, although playing it passably is easier, thanks to all the books, software, and internet resources available today.

One thing that will help speed you along in your study of Omaha is a willingness to let go of most of the lessons you've learned as a hold'em player. Even if you don't muck your hand when someone shows you a singleton King, sooner or later your hold'em background will jump up and bite you, unless you stay vigilant to the dangers of applying Texas hold'em principles to Omaha, named after a city in a neighbouring US state, Nebraska.

While Texas and Nebraska might seem relatively close to someone living in the UK, they might as well be separated by half a world, because there truly is a giant gulf between the two games.

The sooner you realise that, the sooner you can start winning! ❄

WHAT'S ON THE CD?

Everything you need to get you playing online **now**!

VC POKER SOFTWARE DOWNLOAD

Join the poker revolution and play real people from all walks of life and all over the world in VC Poker's friendly poker community.

POKER BALANCE SHEET

If you're going to be a successful poker player, you need to keep a record of your performances and winnings. Use this form to keep a tally.

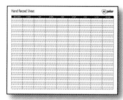

HAND RECORD SHEET

If you make a note of how you played every hand in every betting round, it helps you understand where you're going right and where you fall short.

PLAYER NOTES SHEET

Successful players make observations about other players. Use this form to record things such as other players' starting hands and when they raise or bluff.

HAND ODDS CHART

What are your chances of hitting that straight or flush? Use this chart to calculate whether it's better to play or pass in a given hand.

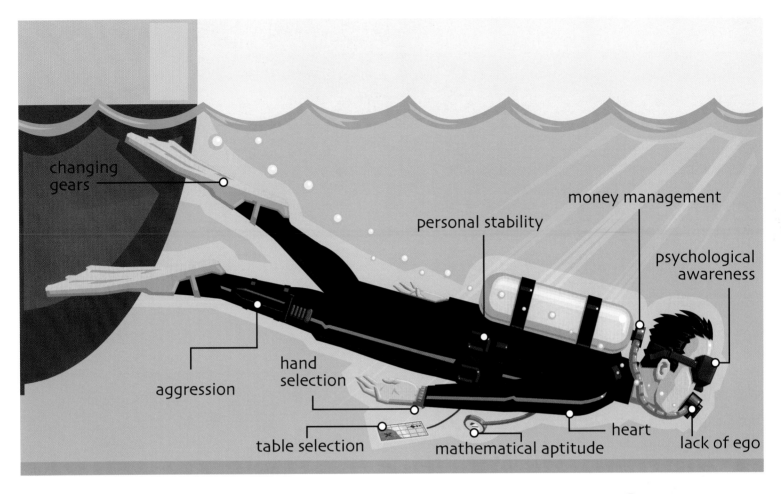

changing gears

money management

personal stability

psychological awareness

aggression

hand selection

table selection

mathematical aptitude

heart

lack of ego

FLOATING TO THE TOP

Poker's vast, murky oceans are littered with the corpses of countless fish, sharks and the odd whale. **Phil Shaw** explains the top ten attributes that successful poker players must be equipped with in order to work their way up the food chain

Pro poker players have a lot to handle to stay at the top of their game, and fall somewhere between professional sportsmen and businessmen.

They succeed in an area where endurance, discipline and skill are paramount, but luck plays a part. But they also often end a day with less capital than they started it with, and so need good money-management skills and the right attitude.

Asked how she coped with the swings, top pro Jennifer Harman replied: 'When I experience a bad beat, I think of it as overhead. If you own a business, you have to pay your bills, and I consider a bad beat one of my bills. It's going to happen, and there's nothing I can do about it.'

Therefore, the purpose of this article is to educate you about the top ten attributes you'll need in order to make it big in the poker world. So, forget how to play J-10 suited in late position for a moment, because sometimes, believe it or not, poker is about everything else but the cards...

1 Table selection

Imagine a Ferrari in a street race, or a donkey in a horse race. It's pretty sure before the off who's going to succeed and who isn't, right? Poker's the same, and if you can consistently find cash games where one or more players is worse than you then over time you're going to be a guaranteed winner.

Forget duelling with the greats at a WPT final table, because this is where the real money is made and, whatever your current level, if you practise good table selection you'll have a consistent earn to progress from, whether it be into bigger cash games or taking shots at tournaments.

How is it done? Well, what you're looking for is weaker players, so getting to know the pros or donkeys in a game or on a site is the obvious way – then just look for one and be

> **If you can consistently find cash games where one or more players is worse than you then over time you're a guaranteed winner**

wary of the other (although if they're as smart as you they might be indicative of a good game). If you're new to a game or site though, then one useful tool of online play is the lobby, where statistics like average pot size or percentage of players seeing the flop can be an indicator. For example, if your game is limit hold'em, then the closer the average pot is to ten big bets (eg $100 in a $5/10 game), the juicier it's likely to be.

2 Money management

Finding great games is all well and good, as long as you can afford the swings that are inevitable in them while your edge accrues. If you see a big game that you can't afford and sit in it, you risk going broke altogether.

Another oft-neglected area is that of keeping records. Businessmen do it, bookies do it, so if you count yourself a serious player then you ➤

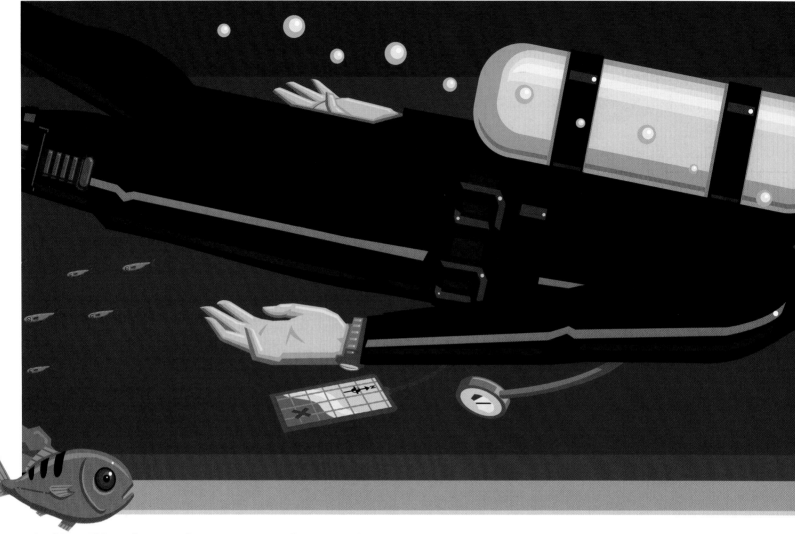

> should too. This can be as simple as writing down how much you've won or lost on a given day so that you know where you are over time, or as complex as also including factors such as hours played, time of day, games and opponents, statistics garnered from the site, and what kind of mood you were in at the time. This way, over time you'll have a little black book that can be used to figure out your optimal playing routine, as well as to tell you how much you're making (or losing) at the game on an hourly rate.

3 Hand selection

So you've found a game that you can afford and promises to offer you a healthy profit. What can you do then to maximise your potential? Well, in most low-limit games the good news is that if you simply wait for better cards than your opponents then you will have a huge edge, as they often play any hand in any position without much thought going into it. Perhaps this is because they're just recreational players, or maybe they've had a few drinks or gone on tilt. But whatever the reason, they're offering you a headstart most of the time, so make sure you take advantage of it.

This is particularly true in limit hold'em games, where the mathematics of position and the fixed-betting structure make imagination and deception less important than in the pot-limit or no-limit varieties, and if you play on the internet it also fits perfectly with multi-tabling. Rather than playing in one game, getting bored and playing every hand, why not play in four at once and wait for those premium hands to come along?

A little black book can be used to figure out your optimal playing routine and to tell you how much you're making (or losing) on an hourly rate

4 Aggression

Once you've gained the discipline to wait for some sort of hand and an understanding of position, you might notice that the other players start to become a bit more cautious of tangling with you. After all, their reasoning goes, if you've entered a pot, you probably have a good reason to be there, right?

Well then, it's time to execute part two of most winning poker players' strategy. Careful hand selection gives you an early edge (making you what's called a 'tight' player), but to capitalise on it you need to be prepared to continue with guns-blazing aggression if you make nothing on the flop or miss a draw, particularly at no-limit or pot-limit. Chances

are, your opponents will have nothing themselves, or give you credit for something strong and fold in the face of your onslaught.

5 Changing gears

So it's tight/aggressive play that mostly brings home the money, but if you stick to one style and play hands in the same way all the time then even your weakest opponents are eventually going to pick up on a few patterns and your edge in a game will start to diminish.

Because of this, most top players have the ability to vary their styles of play to confuse their opponents about what they're up to. In cash games where the structure stays the same this is often done at random – naturally tight players might suddenly play a wider quality or variety of hands and bluff more to steal some extra pots, or loose-aggressive opponents might slow down for a while so that when they get a big hand people don't give them enough credit for it.

In tournaments, changing gears is more dependent on stack size, and what point of the game you're at – eg with a big stack you can open up and bully the opposition, but with a short one you must look for a good hand to go all-in with. But there are still options open to imaginative players – such as playing fast and loose when you're close to

the money and you can see other players are holding on to get there – especially if you care less about the increased risk of getting knocked out than winning the tournament.

6 Heart

Speaking of tournaments, this is what the great players who play just to win have in spades. Have you ever seen someone put their entire stack on the line with a bluff, or overcome a series of terrible beats to seize victory from the jaws of defeat? These are the kind of things poker players mean when they say that someone has 'heart', and if you want to win tournaments you'll need to find some for yourself too, as if you just wait for good cards and hope they'll carry you there, the chances are you'll fall short. As Amir Vahedi once said: 'In order to live, you must be willing to die.'

7 Mathematical aptitude

Whether it's 'A' Level probabilities and combinations or PhDs in Game Theory and Computer Science, most poker pros have a pretty good working knowledge of the mathematics that underpin the game (and the rest have learned the odds by rote or experience). Combined with years of play and seeing the same situations come up again and again, they can understand and estimate very precisely whether certain actions are likely to be profitable or losing plays. Visit a site like *twodimes.net* to get you going.

8 Psychological awareness

Everyone knows that tells (and the people who exhibit them) are key to high-stakes poker and most of the ways they apply to poker have been covered in *Caro's Book of Poker Tells*, so between that and your own experience you'll be well on the way to spotting behavioural patterns. Of course, there is a bigger picture to watch out for as well, such as which players are on tilt, intimidated or showing the traits of a bully, but if you keep your eyes and ears open this will soon be second nature to you and you'll be able to adjust your play accordingly.

9 Lack of ego

When things go wrong, or every move you make seems to work perfectly, it can have a big effect on the way you think about your game or yourself and the other players. But it shouldn't, as you're playing your A game most of the time (hopefully) and the rest should just be the ebb and flow of luck swaying your results back and forth.

But in reality poker players rarely understand the fluctuations they can experience while still being either winning or losing players overall, and so they often end up thinking they're geniuses or doubting their talents. If you can let go of your ego and just focus on the game and the long term rather than how your luck is running, you'll be a mile ahead of many of those who already call themselves professionals.

10 Personal stability

If all this sounds like a lot to contend with then don't worry – it is! Poker is certainly 'a tough way to make an easy living' and you shouldn't attempt to get serious with it unless you think you can tick all the above boxes and more. The history of the game is paved with those who took their shot and missed, and only a small few live to get to the playboy lifestyle and can handle the downswings to keep living it.

This makes emotional wellbeing and the understanding support of your partner, family and friends even more important than usual if you want to give playing seriously a go, and just remember that what was once a fun pastime might soon get stale if you do it every day. If any of this is making you think twice about living the poker life then maybe you should stick with the day job. But if you're still set on sleeping till noon and being your own boss, just make sure the rest of your life is in good order first! ✣

FROM RAGS TO RICHES

Imagine entering a $40 online poker tournie and ending up winning $2.5 million at the WSOP. This has happened – twice. **James Hipwell** reports on the internet poker phenomenon that's back-footing the pros

There were so many people entering this year's World Series of Poker events that it started a debate among the crew of Vegas-based professional players about whether any of them would ever again win a WSOP bracelet. They just couldn't believe how many people they were going to have to beat to get on any one of the 45 final tables from the events making up the WSOP.

With the move to the Amazon Room at Las Vegas' Rio Hotel and Casino, more than 29,000 players stepped up to the felt to compete for in excess of $103 million in prizes that were awarded over the six-week period.

To put that in perspective, it took the previous 35 years for the total prize pool in the WSOP to reach the $300 million in prize money mark. In 2005 alone, one third of that was handed out to the players. The reason? The internet.

With poker mania sweeping the world, a rank amateur can easily rise to the top and become an overnight multi-millionaire at events such as the WSOP. Two years ago, an accountant from Nashville, Tennessee called – unbelievably – Chris Moneymaker

qualified online in a $40 satellite tournament on PokerStars to take the WSOP title – and $2.5 million. Last year, patent lawyer and amateur fossil collector Greg 'Fossilman' Raymer did the same thing, again via qualifying online on PokerStars.

Both players are now big celebrities in the poker scene, which goes some way to explaining why all those people turned up in Vegas this year to compete against the best in the world. In Los Angeles, where Fossilman's face appears on billboards along major thoroughfares, poker players hanging out with their film actor buddies (Jennifer Tilly, Tobey Maguire and Mimi Rogers to name a few) have undergone the bizarre experience of being sought out for their autographs, while their more famous companions are roundly ignored.

For example, Fossilman was walking back to the tournament area from the bathroom at this year's WSOP, but the short walk took almost 15 minutes, as he had to sign 34 autographs and pose for 12 pictures, all the while chatting like a tourist with all who stopped him.

And then there's Moneymaker. Having never played in a real casino

before – indeed, he'd never played the game until he watched the movie *Rounders* – no one gave him a prayer against the 839 others in the Big One. However, a week later, Moneymaker, who had stuck on a cheap hat and mirrored sunglasses to avoid giving away his tells, walked away with the first prize and into the world of overnight celebrity.

Two years on, thousands more dreamers and schemers were in Vegas, hoping to get lucky and make like Moneymaker. During the last two years, he has become a poker pin-up to housewives, truck drivers and college kids alike – if he can win the World Series, they figure, then why not them?

'Yes, I guess I'm the poster boy for online poker,' Moneymaker told a local newspaper at the WSOP this year, shortly before being eliminated in the second round. 'Amateurs and those who had never even played the game watched me on TV and figured, "Hey, I can do that." And they're right.' ➤

With poker mania sweeping the world, a rank amateur can rise to the top and become an overnight multi-millionaire

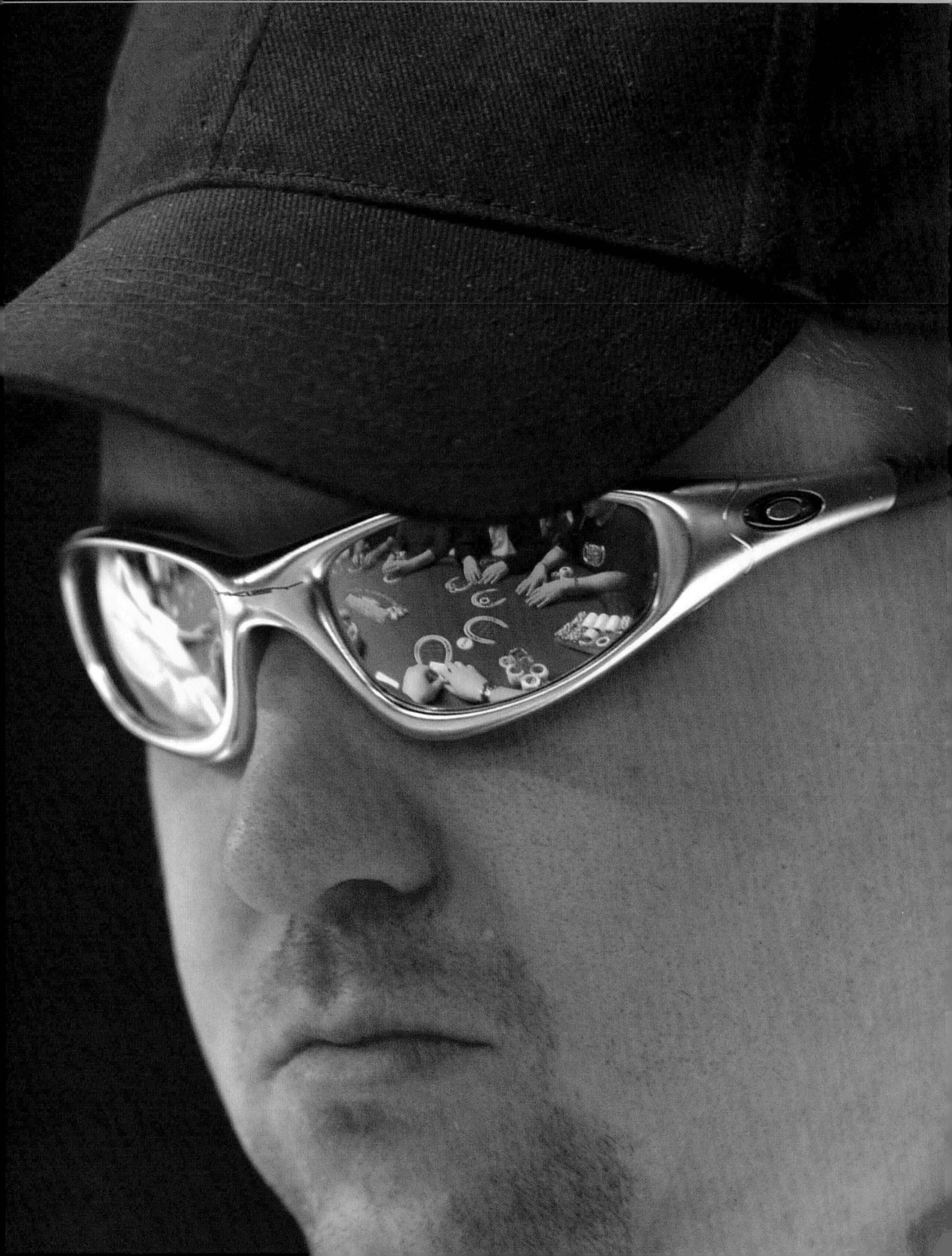

THE MAGIC OF MONEYMAKER

At Binion's Horseshoe in downtown Vegas, where the WSOP main event was held until the poker explosion caused it to outgrow the old casino this year, they held the inaugural World Series product expo.

2003 World Champion Chris Moneymaker walked in with his trademark goatee beard and thousands of fans lined up for an autograph and a photo. An old man, a lifetime of bad beats showing in his face, interrupted Moneymaker. 'I'd just like to say one thing,' the old man said. 'You're the reason for all this.'

'Thank you,' Moneymaker said.

The thing was, you couldn't tell if the old man meant that as a good thing or a bad thing. Chris realises he spawned this madhouse of long shots who enter internet tournaments and dream of becoming millionaires.

'When I won, someone told me it would be the sonic boom of poker,' he said. 'I didn't believe it, but it has been.'

'He is the ultimate amateur,' said Kurt McPhail, co-owner of the Amateur Poker League. 'He proved that if you practise, you can go from nobody to world champion. If it wasn't for Chris, we wouldn't even be here right now.'

➤ Poker has turned into the latest incarnation of the American dream. A century ago, it was the sight of the Statue of Liberty to the incoming immigrant that best symbolised the land of opportunity for all. At the turn of the 21st century, it was buying and selling stocks on the internet in the great dot-com boom. And now it seems to be poker.

Goodbye, Binion's

A decade ago, the WSOP was a discreet little event held at the Binion's Horseshoe casino in downtown Las Vegas, one more money pot among many offered in America's gambling capital. Perhaps 100 players would show up and chip in the $10,000 required to participate. They tended to be pros – strange, febrile, driven individuals with colourful pasts often involving drugs, booze or chillingly close run-ins with mafioso loan sharks. Then up popped the internet. The first online poker sites made their debut in 1998, the same year that *Rounders*, a poker movie starring Ed Norton and Matt Damon, became a modest box-office hit. Suddenly it was possible for people all over the world to hone their Texas hold'em skills in

front of a computer without feeling like they were risking the house, or the kids' college fund.

By 2000, the winning pot at the WSOP topped $1 million. In 2003, poker started to be broadcast on US TV, modestly at first on the Travel Channel on cable, and then with an increasing frenzy on CBS's sports channel, Fox's sports channel and, finally, on sports station ESPN.

It might not seem like the most obvious of spectator sports, but the Travel Channel pioneered a way of making it more dramatic by editing the games down to their most tense moments and using hidden cameras to show the TV audience what no live spectator could see – the hole cards held by each player.

Fruit of the boom

Since 2003, the game has exploded. When the Travel Channel first began its broadcasts, online poker sites worldwide were attracting about 88,000 players betting just under $16 million each day. As of May this year, those numbers had mushroomed to 1.8 million players risking $200 million each day online.

UK viewers can watch poker at most times of the day or night on channels such as Challenge TV, Bravo and the Travel Channel. We even have two dedicated poker TV channels – the Poker Channel and PokerZone – neither of which would have been deemed viable even two years ago.

For sites such as VC Poker, PartyPoker and PokerStars, it's 1999 all over again. PartyPoker has even

been floated on the London Stock Exchange with a price tag of £5 billion, making its founders billionaires.

These websites have so many users paying to compete against each other, they can afford to sponsor loads of players at the WSOP and, sometimes, offer other inducements as well.

Around 1,100 players qualified for the main event via PokerStars this year – approximately 20% of the entries. Paradise Poker even gave its top ten contestants a free tropical holiday as well as travel, hotel and spending money.

Meanwhile, at VC Poker, each of the qualifiers for the main event were treated to a night out with Doyle 'Texas Dolly' Brunson, the legendary poker player and author of *Super System*, the most famous poker book ever published. Presumably, the pep talk must have worked, as two of the VC Poker qualifiers got into the money.

The numbers really are staggering. At the WSOP main event this year, 5,619 players turned up to compete for a prize pot of $52 million. The first prize was a cool $7.5 million, while second place won $4.25 million. Meanwhile, a finish in the top ten made you an instant millionaire, and a top-100 finish earned you $77,000.

Technologists and other experts all talked about the internet being the vehicle for a new industrial order, which, with hindsight, was something of an exaggeration. But it sure as hell has worked for poker! ✿

> **Suddenly it was possible for people all over the world to hone their Texas hold'em skills in front of a computer**

Join the poker room that holds all the aces.

Join the poker revolution with VC Poker and get more than just the chance to play poker. Instead, why not join the poker room that offers clear, easy-to-use software, a market leading loyalty programme and games and tournaments that let you play for the levels you want, when you want.

vcpoker.com

Victor Chandler

BEST POKER SCENE OF ALL TIME

In *Rounders*, Mike is pondering what he's going to do now that his girlfriend has walked out on him and Worm chimes in with: 'You know what cheers me up when I'm feeling sh*tty? Rolled up Aces over Kings. Yeah, check-raising stupid tourists and taking huge pots off 'em. Stacks and towers of chips I can't see over. Playin' all-night high-limit hold'em at the Taj... where the sand turns to gold...'

Mike says: 'F*ck it, let's go,' to which Worm replies: 'Don't tease me.'

'Let's play some f*ckin' cards,' Mike responds, with feeling.

Off they go to the Taj, with Mike narrating, 'If a fish acts strong, he's bluffing. If he acts weak, he's got a hand, it's that simple.'

Hollywood or bust

Poker's allure has proved irresistible to filmmakers from Hollywood's origins to Miramax's dedicated poker film *Rounders*, made in 1998. But out of all the films involving poker ever made, which are the best? **James Hipwell** has seen them all

It is a long tradition of Hollywood that it uses gambling, and more often than not poker, to add flavour to a film. Unfortunately some of these films have silly scenes (like *House of Games*) or are genuinely awful (mentioning no names *Honeymoon in Vegas*) or indeed both (*Maverick*). But there are some good ones, too, and if you're getting into poker there are a few movies that you will soon come to regard as unmissable.

Below is our list of the six best motion pictures that include card playing scenes:

The Cincinnati Kid (1965)
Game Five-card stud
Plot It's 1920s/30s New Orleans and a new kid has come to town to beat the notorious Lancey Howard (Edward

Robinson), the best poker player in the country. With the help of an old friend and card dealer, Eric Stoner (Steve McQueen) manages to get in on the highest stakes game of his life. *The Cincinnati Kid* is all about the poker scene at the end, which is one of the best ever captured on celluloid.

However, you must sit through some flat performances about revenge and romance to get there. There are a couple of good moments of sexual tension between McQueen and Ann Margret (playing Melba) in between Steve truly wanting to be with Christian (Tuesday Weld).
Poker comment Like *Rounders* this is for

▲ In the high-stakes world of poker portrayed in *Rounders*, Mike (Matt Damon) sets out to prove he plays by skill, not luck

'Listen, here's the thing. If you can't spot the sucker in your first half-hour at the table, *you are* the sucker'

poker aficionados. Probably the most famous poker movie of all time although the pros will tell you the finale is ludicrous.
Best line 'That's what it's all about – doing the wrong thing at the right time.'
Dig rating ♠♠♠♠

The Sting (1973)
Game Five-card stud
Plot When you play a cheater, be sure you cheat better than he does. Set in 1936, *The Sting* is about a pair of Chicago con artists (Paul Newman and Robert Redford) who find themselves in a high-stakes game against the master of all cheating mobsters (Shaw) when they set out to avenge the murder of a mutual friend and partner. Using a bogus bookie joint as a front for their con of all cons, the two

feel the heat from the Chicago Mob on one side and encroaching police on the other. But in a plot that contains more twists than a treacherous mountain road, the ultimate scam is pulled off with consummate style and panache.
Poker comment The poker scene on the train is one of the best poker scenes ever shot, although it's more about cheating than real poker.
Best line 'Not only are you a cheat – you're a gutless cheat.'
Dig rating ♠♠♠

Lock, Stock and Two Smoking Barrels (1998)
Game Brag
Plot Cockney boys Tom, Soap, Eddie, and Bacon are in a bind: they owe seedy criminal and porn king 'Hatchet' Harry a sizable amount of cash after

Eddie loses half a million in a high-stakes game of poker that's been rigged by Hatchet. Hot on their tails is a thug named Big Chris, who intends to send them all to the hospital if they don't come up with the cash in the allotted time. Before long, the boys are caught up in a labyrinth of double-crosses that lead to a multitude of dead bodies, copious amounts of drugs, and two antique rifles.
Poker comment Does its best to promote brag at a time when interest in Texas hold'em is seemingly unstoppable.
Best line Don: 'I'll fold.' Phil: 'Fold? Is that the only word you learnt at school?'
Dig rating ♠♠♠♠

Kaleidoscope (1966)
Game Five-card stud
Plot Barney (played by Warren Beatty) breaks into a factory and doctors the plates that print the playing cards used by the major casinos of the world. He marks the cards in a way only he can see. Naturally, after these cards go into circulation, Beatty goes on the 'rush' to end all rushes playing blackjack and poker. Unfortunately for him, when forced into a heads-up no-limit game, they switch cards to ones he can't read. Now forced to play using only his wits, he traps his opponent into an enormous pot, only to be faced with the best poker decision ever caught on film.
Poker comment A crude film based on Ian Fleming's *Casino Royale* but with some poker scenes worth seeing.
Best line None worth repeating but the film's catchline was: 'Love. Larceny. Luck. They're all in the cards.'
Dig rating ♠♠♠

California Split (1974)
Games Texas hold'em
Plot Though dated, this is the only movie that has ever attempted to show the day-to-day life of card-playing, sports-betting, sleep-till-noon gamblers. Marred only by a poor ending and muddled sound, *California Split* was directed by Robert Altman (who made *The Player*). George Segal and Elliot Gould play Gardena poker players in search of a rush. Legendary gambler and former WSOP main event winner Amarillo Slim also appears.
Poker comment Self-consciously arty as you would expect from Altman, which is appropriate given that poker can be a beautiful game.
Best line 'I feel like a winner, but I know I look like a loser.'
Dig rating ♠♠♠

Rounders (1998)
Game Texas hold'em
Plot Matt Damon is the level-headed Mike McDermott who insists he can beat the game and make it into the upper echelon of tournament poker in Vegas. The film opens with that dream coming to a crashing halt at the hands of Teddy KGB (John Malkovich), who takes every penny Mike has in a real 'blood game'. Devastated, Mike vows to quit the game forever, but his best friend, the nauseating Worm (Ed Norton), coaxes him back into the addiction. The film makes the case that some of us are born with certain passions and we should follow them.
Poker comment Will fire your interest in the game, probably forever.
Best line 'Listen, here's the thing. If you can't spot the sucker in your first half-hour at the table, then *you are* the sucker...' (There are at least another 20 great one-liners. Listen out for Worm's theory about women being the 'rake'.)
Dig rating ♠♠♠♠♠

7 of the best poker one-liners from the silver screen

★ *Three Godfathers* (1936). Several film versions of this story exist, the best being the 1948 version with John Wayne. In this version, after Walter Brennan helps a stranger cheat at poker, the stranger asks, 'Why did you do that?' Brennan replies: 'I dunno. I guess I'm just a no-good rat.'

★ *Run* (1990). Patrick Dempsey kills time at an illegal card game in New Jersey before legalisation of casino poker there. Here we get a rare filmed record of a player tipping the dealer, and the waving off of obnoxious second-hand smoke. The game climaxes when a belligerent, violent player forces Dempsey to draw one card instead of standing pat. 'This is a new twist: Gestapo poker.'

★ *The Gunfighter* (1950). One of the all-time best serious Westerns, Gregory Peck stars as a notorious gunfighter who only wants to settle down to a calm life, but is endlessly pestered by every little squirt in the world looking to make a reputation for himself. Despite the serious theme, there are two hysterical scenes. One features two old guys fighting (after a poker dispute). A third one, watching, says, 'I've seen better fights than this in a prayer meeting.' The brief poker scene features the old men playing poker in the local barbershop. When a new man walks in, they try to persuade him to join the game. The new man says, 'I wouldn't sit in this game with cards I made myself.'

★ *The Gambler From Natchez* (1954) 'How did you know he was bluffing?' 'He kept looking back at his hole cards. If you got it, you don't need to keep looking back to see what you got.'

★ *Cheyenne Autumn* ((1964) (Wyatt Earp to Doc Holliday discussing what to do with a card cheat in their three-handed game): 'If we shoot him, we won't have anyone to play with.'

★ *Dr Mabuse* (1922): 'It's always been a dream of youthful ambition, to win at cards and love.'

★ *Robin and the Seven Hoods* (1964): 'When your opponent's holding all the Aces, there's only one thing to do. Kick over the table.'

Lights, camera... poker

Hollywood has always been a poker town – perhaps *the* poker town. The biggest names in the film industry have always been fond of late-night, big-money card games. The difference now, explains **James Hipwell**, is that celebrities are doing it in the public eye

For over 50 years celebrities – and we're talking not just C-listers but those at the very zenith of Hollywood society – have been in love with the game of poker. In the past many have proved themselves useless, indulging their passion more in fun than seriousness, but these days film stars such as Ben Affleck, Matt Damon, Tobey Maguire and Mimi Rogers are competing at the highest level. They have found they can hold their own, not just in televised games such as *Celebrity Poker Showdown*, but even among the world's top players in Los Angeles-based pro/am tournaments.

The game has come a long way since film stars over several generations met up in home games more to get drunk, compare bankrolls and escape the wife or lover for a few hours than to play serious poker.

Walter Mathau used to hold a weekly home game but would spend more time listening to the night's big baseball game on the radio – upon which he invariably had a massive bet – than concentrating on the cards. People who played with him said this apparent indifference was his major strength. Meanwhile, across town film director John Huston used tequila as the route to success in his home game.

Dutch courage

'We used to play in the afternoon. It was a pot-limit five-card stud game that started at 12, and at one o'clock, he would say, "Gentlemen – it's time for our tequila",' says former actor Vince Van Patten, one of Huston's poker buddies who now commentates on the World Poker Tour.

This wasn't long before Huston's death and he was on a respirator at the time. Like it or not, you had to shoot a major shot of tequila with him.

'After that, the game would totally loosen up, and you'd notice that everybody was playing sloppy. But not Huston, whose judgment appeared to be unimpaired. He seemed to rake in all the money after that but he would tell great stories about Bogart,' remembers Patten.

The home games that have been legion in the hills around Hollywood for several decades have come on a stage since then thanks to big-name film stars such as Ben Affleck and Tobey Maguire. The *Pearl Harbour* actor and former beau of J-Lo moved into the big time by winning $356,000 in the 2004 California State Poker Championship at the Commerce Casino, while another household name

Tobey 'Spiderman' Maguire took nearly 100,000 bucks for first place in a Phil Hellmuth Invitational at Hollywood Park in October 2004.

The celebrity poker craze has been driven in the US by two competing and very successful TV shows – *Celebrity Poker Showdown* on Bravo and *The Hollywood Home Game* (presented by Patten) on Travel Channel. The craze has reached the UK too with *Celebrity Poker Club* a ratings success on Challenge TV and a host of celebrities turning up on both the Ladbrokes Poker Million (aired on Sky) and the British Poker Open on the newly-launched Poker Channel.

One of the hosts on *Celebrity Poker Showdown* is a somewhat cheesy professional player with over-bleached teeth called Phil Gordon, who has been able to boost his $1.2m of tournament winnings by commentating on the celebrity play. He even admits to fleecing some of the Tinseltown contingent, saying: 'Quite often, I'm lucky enough to get these guys in a cash game at filming.'

Gordon says there are good reasons why Hollywood has taken to poker.

'It's a very compelling game and the psychological aspects are very appealing to people in the acting profession who, most of the time, have to get into character.'

But there are reasons too why even an A-lister's acting skills might not stand up to the stare-down of a professional player.

> **'The psychological aspects are appealing to people in the acting profession who have to get into character'**

'For those that know how to do it well, it could be an advantage but actors can be at a disadvantage too,' explains Gordon.

Hamming it up

'One of the things that I find funny about playing with these guys is that, because they act, they over-act and they're very easy to read because of that. It's very easy to pick up whether they have a good hand or a bad hand. But the ones that have caught on like Affleck are very good at not displaying any emotion – which is acting in itself.'

In the UK there is a well trodden path to TV studios in Cardiff where the last two series of *Celebrity Poker Club* have been filmed. Not that you find Jude Law or Hugh Grant lining up just yet. At the moment it's more Borehamwood than Hollywood. The roll-call for the last series featured ex-cricketers, snooker players, a bevvy of young TV presenters, former boy-banders, most of the actors from Channel 4's *Teachers*, some comedians and John McCririck, who would turn up for the opening of an envelope!

Thanks to Chris Moneymaker, who won the World Series of Poker main event ($2.5m) in 2003 – after qualifying via a $40 internet tournament – poker players themselves are attaining celebrity status. When Ben Affleck met Scotty Nguyen, one of the best poker players in the world, he responded in the same way people usually respond to him…'My God, I can't believe it's…' The star power of Affleck, it seemed, was eclipsed for a moment by the poker might of Nguyen. Then again, Affleck could have been acting.

▼ Ah, the glamour of celebrity poker. But who's the chap in the suit beside the UK's favourite racing pundit, John McCririck?

Joseph Hachem with 7.5m of his new best friends

Gus Hansen failed to cash in this time

Doyle 'Texas Dolly' Brunson can't help feeling Superman has let himself go a bit

Down to the last two in the 2005 WSOP main event

It could happen to YOU!

The WSOP main event is the Holy Grail for poker players. Previous winners have become legends, while recent winners have provided 'if he can do it, I can, too' fairytales. **James Hipwell** followed the action at this year's tournament

As the sun started to creep up above the Nevada skyline at 6.46am on 15 July 2005, a turn of a card changed Joseph Hachem's life forever. Hachem, a former chiropractor from Australia, had been playing almost non-stop no-limit Texas hold'em for 14 hours on the final day of the WSOP main event when he decided to go all-in against American Steve Dannenmann.

Hachem had flopped a straight, his opponent missed the chance to split the pot on the river, and suddenly the Aussie was a whopping $7.5 million richer. As the fellow countrymen who had boisterously supported him throughout launched into chants of 'Aussie, Aussie, Aussie! Oi! Oi! Oi!' the 38-year-old took a joyous victory lap around the stage at Binion's Horseshoe and wrapped himself in an Australian flag.

That's why they call it the 'Big One'
This had been a classic showdown in the finest traditions of the WSOP. This year's main event was so big the organisers

switched most of the action from Binion's, the slightly raffish casino in downtown Las Vegas, where it had been held every year since the tournament's inception in 1970, to the smarter and altogether more capacious Rio casino and hotel off the Strip, only returning to its old venue for the final table.

The explosion in the popularity of poker was evident in the increase in the field of entrants. A throng of 5,619 hopefuls had together staked an incredible $52 million for their chance of glory. The number of participants was more than double the 2,576 of last year and almost seven times the then-record 839 players who entered in 2003, when the almost magically named (for PR purposes anyway) Chris Moneymaker triumphed. This year's tournament certainly showed just why the WSOP main event was

Annie Duke didn't make it to day two

Anyone know the collective noun for dealer buttons?

Chris 'Jesus' Ferguson with his sponsored stetson

Tobey 'Spiderman' Maguire looking short stacked

From now on, he'll be known as Hach the Cash...

If I cover my ears, eyes and head, you really won't be able to read my tells

set up as a foundation for a world championship and why the winner can justifiably call himself World Champion.

Setting their sites

At least half of the players in this year's main event qualified online at sites such as VC Poker. Indeed, WSOP main event final table competitors Aaron Kanter and Andrew Black qualified online with a poker site.

Kanter, from California, who finished fourth, won his seat through a tournament from just a $12 investment, while fifth-placed

> **At least half of the players in this year's WSOP main event qualified online at sites such as VC Poker**

Black qualified on a $300+$28 satellite.

Of course, the WSOP's 'Big One' isn't the only opportunity to qualify for globally televised tournaments with huge cash prizes. Both the World Poker Tour and the European Poker Tour obtain most of their entrants through internet satellites, proving that it really does pay to regularly check sites like *vcpoker.com* for details.

Back with 2005's main event, all the colourful poker characters had shown up at the Rio, including Doyle 'Texas Dolly' Brunson, Phil 'The Brat' Hellmuth, Daniel 'Kid Poker'

Negreanu, Chris 'Jesus' Ferguson, Phil 'The Unabomber' Laak, Antonio 'The Magician' Esfandiari, Dave 'Devilfish' Ulliott and Greg 'Fossilman' Raymer. They joined a couple of thousand online aficionados who each aspired to make their fame and fortune.

Enter the A-list

There was no shortage of celebrities, either. Confirmed poker fans and Hollywood stars Shannon Elizabeth, James Woods, Tobey Maguire, Jennifer Tilly, Mimi Rogers and, er, Stephen Hendry – not to mention the many who have played on *Celebrity Poker Showdown* – have all given the game a certain cool cachet.

'I play every single day of the year – in private games, casinos and online,' says Woods, who lasted 11.5 hours in the first round of the main event before he exited ➤

When I said 'Fold'em', I didn't mean literally...

Greg 'Fossilman' Raymer came 25th this year and took $304,680 back to Connecticut

Daniel Bergsdorf of Sweden eyes Mike the Mouth's chip stack

A British bulldog looks pleased with his effort

Mike 'The Mouth' Matusow gets busted off the final table, taking with him a million bucks

Any of you f****** pricks move, and I'll execute every m************ last one of ya!

> on the first Saturday night. 'I read about it. I'm very committed to it. I'm passionate about it. It's a challenge to your mind, your soul. You've got to be an artist and a scientist to play poker well. I'm a little of both.'

Asked whether his acting skills help him bluff, Woods says: 'It's more how I read other people. I know if they're telling me the truth. I'm a director, too, so when I watch people, I can tell when they're lying. It's one of my strengths.'

The WSOP, buzzing with celebrities and fans (or railbirds as they're known in Vegas) pressing in behind the ropes, felt more like the Academy Awards than a poker tournament. It was a day-and-night party

Every one of the nine brave souls who faced poker's ultimate test acquitted himself with honour at this year's WSOP main event

that ended not just with one guy going home with $7.5 million, but also a no-limit hold'em title worth millions in endorsements and a platinum, diamond and ruby bracelet that will intimidate opponents for years.

Taking the strain

Imagine what it must feel like to reach the final table of the Big One. Start by imagining you're physically, mentally, and emotionally exhausted (if not exhausted, at the least quite drained).

Add into the mix that a chance of a lifetime (for most people) has presented itself to you. Next, sprinkle in some unfamiliar surroundings, and the knowledge that while only a few hundred people will be watching

live as you play your game, tens of thousands of your peers and millions of spectators are later, through the magic of televised hole cards, going to dissect every effort you make, praising you when you succeed, but also look upon you with disdain if you make the slightest error. Just for kicks, add pure chance, which can at any moment jump up and ruin your best efforts, with no 'justice' or 'fairness' involved.

To pursue the ultimate goal, you'll not merely have to conquer the world's toughest foe (yourself), but you'll have to outwit eight skilled individuals who want the prize just as much as you do – and maybe some of them want it even more.

It's Lady Luck and you against the world, or the world and Lady Luck against you. What a potential dream; what a potential nightmare; what a rush.

Shuffle up and deal... er... where is everyone?

Tiffany Williamson of London's Gutshot Club was the last woman standing and won $400,000 for coming 15th

Joseph Hachem and Steve Dannenmann seconds after the tournament ended

Irishman Andrew 'The Monk' Black (left) and bar owner John 'Tex' Barch came fifth and third respectively

Brad Kondracki gets eliminated in eighth place, but a $1.15m sweetener makes life more comfortable

Every one of the nine brave souls who faced poker's ultimate test acquitted himself with honour and distinction at this year's WSOP. The game's very nature – the turn of a card, the fact that someone *must* finish ninth and someone *must* finish eighth and someone *must* finish first – meant each competitor had to leave the table in a unique position, some much more desirable than others, but years from now, when the subject of the 2005 WSOP main event final table comes up, anyone who was part of it should be able to speak of his effort with pride.

The final countdown

Certainly, Joseph Hachem will have a few poker yarns to tell his mates back in his native Melbourne, although not many of them will be bad beat stories.

For 14 hours, Hachem and Dannenmann had outsmarted a stellar group at the final table. Mike Matusow, a professional player based in Las Vegas, was favoured to win after finishing sixth in 2001 and 87th last year. However, he was the first of the finalists to be eliminated, a setback softened by the $1 million paycheque he earned for finishing in ninth place.

The other finalists reflected the cross-cultural appeal of poker. Brad Kondracki, 24, a law student at Pennsylvania, finished eighth; Daniel Bergsdorf, a truck driver from Sweden, was seventh; Scott Lazar, 42, who works on independent films and is a professional magician, was sixth; Andrew 'The Monk' Black, 39, a Buddhist charity worker from Dublin, whose hobbies include ➤

CHIP COUNTS

Chip counts going on to the final table	
Aaron Kanter	10,700,000
John 'Tex' Barch	9,330,000
Andrew Black	8,140,000
Mike Matusow	7,410,000
Steve Dannenmann	5,460,000
Joseph Hachem	5,420,000
Daniel Bergsdorf	5,270,000
Scott Lazar	3,370,000
Brad Kondracki	1,180,000

Viva Las Vegas! This player got married the day before the main event started

Xuyen 'Badgirl' Pham on day one of the 2005 WSOP main event

Brad Kondracki examines his hole cards

Aaron Kanter was chip leader going onto the final table, but finished fourth

Greg Raymer sings a version of a Britney Spears song entitled, 'Oops, I nearly did it again'

WSOP 2005 RESULTS

Results of the 2005 World Series of Poker main event, with winnings

1st	Joseph Hachem	$7.5 million
2nd	Steve Dannenmann	$4.25 million
3rd	John 'Tex' Barch	$2.5 million
4th	Aaron Kanter	$2 million
5th	Andrew Black	$1.75 million
6th	Scott Lazar	$1.5 million
7th	Daniel Bergsdorf	$1.3 million
8th	Brad Kondracki	$1.15 million
9th	Mike Matusow	$1 million

➤ 'contemplation and meditation', came fifth; Aaron Kanter, 27, a former loan officer from California, was fourth, while John 'Tex' Barch, 34, who owns a bar in Texas, finished third.

For much of the final rounds, Hachem was among the short stacks at the table. At one point, he was down to 2.5 million in chips. Still, he stuck to his strategy, which was to play small pots and avoid risking all of his chips. It was the opposite approach of Dannenmann, who frequently raised all-in throughout the exhausting session.

'A million would have changed everything, let alone $7.5 million'

Dannenmann, a mortgage banker from California, didn't look too disappointed with second place: he hugged his wife having just made $4.5 million. By the end, as he later admitted, he 'just wanted it to end'.

Hachem if you can

Here are the last few stages of how Hachem won the 2005 WSOP main event (not to mention a cool $7.5m).

Dannenmann had the button, he raised to $700,000, and Hachem called. The flop came 6♥, 5♦, 4♦, Hachem checked, and

After 14 hours of solid poker, massages were a must-have

Joseph Hachem invokes the Aboriginal gods of his homeland... and wins

Olga Varkonyi, wife of 2002 WSOP main event champion Robert, came 238th this year

The Mouth airs his pits after sweating it out at the final table

If you see one of these around a poker table in Vegas, run for the hills

Dannenmann bet $700,000. Hachem raised to $1.7 million and Dannenmann called. The turn card was the A♠, Hachem bet $2 million, Dannenmann slowly raised to $5 million, Hachem re-raised all-in and Dannenmann immediately called. Hachem showed 7♣-3♦ (7-high straight), while Dannenmann had A♦-3♣ (top pair). Dannenmann needed to catch a 7 on the river to chop the pot with equal straights.

The entire crowd was on their feet as the river card came. There were only three cards that could keep Hachem from becoming champion. The river was 4♣! Joseph Hachem had just become the 2005 World Series of Poker champion and winner of a once-in-a-lifetime pot.

'A million would have changed my life, let alone $7.5 million,' said Hachem. 'It changes everything.' ✿

IT'S ALL ABOUT THE BRACELETS

Although the $10,000 buy-in, no-limit hold'em event is the one that decides who is World Champion, there are 44 other events played in Vegas over six weeks from the beginning of June to the middle of July that make up the World Series of Poker. For every one of these events, the winner is awarded a spectacular bracelet, and these are much coveted.

When this year's WSOP began, three men were tied at the top of the WSOP bracelet list. Doyle 'Texas Dolly' Brunson, Johnny Chan and Phil 'The Brat' Hellmuth, all legends in their own right, had nine each, and no one imagined that this situation would change. But it did.

The first player to shake the standings was Johnny Chan. Early in the morning of 27 June, Chan came down to the final two in the $2,500 pot-limit hold'em event with Phil 'The Unabomber' Laak. In what was

one of the fastest heads-up showdowns of the tournament, Chan vanquished The Unabomber in 17 hands to capture his tenth bracelet. History was made.

Wristful thinking

Not so fast, though. Not to be outdone, four days later, Texas Dolly, now in his 70s, overcame a demanding final table in the $5,000 no-limit, short-handed event to take his tenth bracelet as well. Along the way, he outlasted two former fellow World Champions, Scotty Nguyen and Chris 'Jesus' Ferguson, as well as Layne Flack, Men 'The Master' Nguyen and Minh Ly.

The Brat was unable to reply to either of them. While cashing in several events, he made only one final table and was eliminated in eighth place in that event, so he has to look up to the leaders in the 'Bracelet Race', Texas Dolly and Chan.

Mind your language

If you don't know your Siegfried & Roy from your German Lesbians, don't despair. We reveal the nicknames of starting poker hands

If you've ever been at a poker table feeling on top of things when the other players started speaking in tongues, using words such as 'Flat Tyres', 'Doggie Balls' and 'Big Chick', you'll know what it feels like to be uncool. Just for you, then, here's some common and not-so-common names for starting poker hands.

A-A	Pocket Rockets, American Airlines, Bullets
A-K	Big Slick
A-Q	Little Slick, Big Chick
A-8	Dead Man's Hand (the hand held by Wild Bill Hickok when he was shot)
A-3	Ashtray, Baskin Robbins
K-K	Cowboys, King Kong
K-Qos	Mixed Marriage
K-Qs	Marriage
K-J	Kojak, King John
K-9	A pair of dogs (as in canine), Fido
Q-Q	Siegfried & Roy, Ladies, Four Tits
Q-J	Maverick
Q-7	Computer Hand (from an apocryphal story that a computer proved these were the most commonly occurring cards on the flop)
Q-3	Gay Waiter, San Francisco waiter (queen with a tray)
J-J	Knaves, Hooks, Fishhooks, Jay Birds
J-A	Jackass, Ajax
J-5	Motown, Jackson Five
J-4	Flat Tyres (as in what's a Jack for?)
10-10	Dimes
10-5	Woolworth's (because it was traditionally a chain of 5- and 10-cent stores), Five & Dime
10-4	Over And Out, Roger That, Convoy, Good Buddy
10-2	Doyle Brunson (because he became World Champion twice with this hand)
9-8	Oldsmobile
9-9	German Lesbian/Virgin (as in 'Nein, Nein'), Popeyes, Phil Hellmuth
9-5	Dolly Parton
9-2	Montana Banana (said to refer to it being more likely that bananas will grow in chilly Montana than this hand making money)
8-8	Snowmen, Two Fat Ladies, Doggie Balls
7-7	Sunset Strip, Mullets, Saturn, Hockey Sticks
7-8	RPM
7-6	Union Oil
7-2	Beer Hand (if you're playing poker's worst hand, it's time for a beer)
6-6	Route 66, Kicks
6-9	Big Lick, Dinner For Two, The Good Lover
5-5	Speed Limit, Presto
4-4	Diana Dors, Magnum
4-5	Jesse James, Colt 45
3-9	Jack Benny (refers to a running gag about the late US comic's age)
3-8	Raquel Welch (said to refer to the size of the *One Million Years B.C.* actress' most impressive assets)
3-3	Crabs (looks like two crustaceans on their sides)
2-2	Ducks, Pocket Swans